Wicked Kansas

Adrian Zink

Published by The History Press
Charleston, SC
www.historypress.com

Copyright © 2019 by Adrian Zink
All rights reserved

First published 2019

Manufactured in the United States

ISBN 9781467143882

Library of Congress Control Number: 2019948152

Notice: The information in this book is true and complete to the best of our knowledge. It is offered without guarantee on the part of the author or The History Press. The author and The History Press disclaim all liability in connection with the use of this book.

All rights reserved. No part of this book may be reproduced or transmitted in any form whatsoever without prior written permission from the publisher except in the case of brief quotations embodied in critical articles and reviews.

I dedicate this book to all the people out there who enjoy hearing and telling great stories. Life is richer and less monotonous with people like you around.

CONTENTS

Preface   7

1. Murderers, Gunfighters and Serial Killers   9
2. Secret Lives   35
3. Politics   46
4. Vigilante Justice   64
5. The Passions of War   70
6. Thieves   76
7. Con Artists   84

Bibliography   89
About the Author   96

PREFACE

Amelia Earhart soared into international fame as a trailblazing aviator and icon. Dwight D. Eisenhower led millions of soldiers as the supreme Allied commander in World War II and later served as the thirty-fourth president of the United States. Walter P. Chrysler founded of one of the "Big Three" U.S. automobile manufacturers. What all of these Kansans have in common are the positive contributions they gave to the world and their lofty places in nearly every Kansas history book. It's not wrong that we should look up to such people and mention their influence on our modern world. The constant lionization of people like them serves to highlight the positive aspects of a place like Kansas, but it also leads to the question, "What about the not-so-great people?"

The world isn't all made up of saints. If it were, we wouldn't need police, prisons, locks on our homes and cars and warnings to our children about "stranger danger." Though we all intrinsically know that, we don't see the rotten side of humanity very often in history books about Kansas. Of course, we have plenty of discussion about John Brown, but he was a very important historical figure to the pre–Civil War hostilities of the territory. No mention of him would be a massive oversight. What about other less heralded people who were just...wicked? Where do we put them in our history books?

I came across the inspiration for this book by accident while working on my first book, *Hidden History of Kansas*. I noticed that the more Kansas history I read, the more sordid murderers, con artists and just plain bad people I kept coming across in the old accounts, diaries and newspapers. I included

Preface

some of their stories in that book, covering outlaws like the Dalton Gang and Bonnie and Clyde. I did not, however, focus too much of my attention on the underbelly of humanity. I decided to let those stories pile up on the side for a later work, and now they have a proper home in *Wicked Kansas*.

"Wickedness" can be defined in a number of ways depending on who you are talking to. It is similar to the word "evil" or the term "morally wrong" to some people. To others, it could be someone who is simply extremely unpleasant or who intends to inflict harm on others. The word could also indicate a more lighthearted soul inhabited with a playful mischievousness in them. In this work, the term is used loosely and can mean every one of those and more. It's up to the reader to determine just how wicked these characters are as you take this journey down the seedier side of Kansas history. It's a place inhabited by drunken killers, pimps, escaped convicts, drug kingpins, petty thieves, quack doctors, serial killers and just plain rotten characters. I hope you enjoy the rubbernecking as much as I have.

I owe special thanks to my editor, Lindsey Givens, who has helped me stay focused and confident on this sophomore effort of mine. I would also like to thank Lauren Gray at the Kansas Historical Society for her expertise in helping me select and scan the right images for this work. A big thanks is also due to Jonathan Trackwell, who was my first reader and helped me smooth out my prose. My copyeditor, Hayley Behal, also kept my writing consistent, and I much appreciate her advice! Lastly, I'd like to give special recognition to Mike Nieken at Arcadia Publishing. Mike was instrumental in helping me every step of the way with my sales of the first book. This work was a true collaboration, and I couldn't have done it alone.

1
MURDERERS, GUNFIGHTERS AND SERIAL KILLERS

THE BLOODY BENDERS:
SERIAL KILLERS ON THE HIGH PRAIRIE

In 1865—after the traumatic early years of Kansas's history with the border violence and the subsequent Civil War—the state opened up for eager settlers to the now-peaceful land. The Homestead Act of 1862 drove waves upon waves of settlers to the state, with 160 acres provided to anyone willing to work the land for five years. Southeastern Kansas was also open for settlement now, as the Osage Indians moved to the Indian Territory in what is now the Oklahoma Panhandle. Many hardy homesteaders from Northern Europe came to tame the land, including a family who would become notorious in state lore: The Benders.

Two German immigrants, a middle-aged father and mid-twenties son, John Bender Sr. and John Bender Jr. came down the Osage Trail—a rough wagon trail cutting southwest from Fort Scott to Independence. Seeing an opportunity to stake a claim in this area, they decided to purchase land right on the trail in Labette County, northeast of Cherryvale. They set to work building their own home, which included lumber from Fort Scott for the frame and sandstone blocks for the foundation in the newly dug cellar under the house, as well as a stable, pens, a corral and a well. By the spring of 1871, they were ready to send for the women of the family, "Ma" Bender and sister Kate, who was twenty.

Sketch of John Bender Sr. between 1870–79. *Courtesy of Kansas Historical Society.*

With large numbers of travelers passing through the trail on the way to Indian Territory, Texas and beyond, there was ample opportunity to make money by selling general goods. The grocery supplied food, tools, clothing, blankets, tobacco and pretty much anything else you would find in a general store at the time. The Bender family's one-room home was divided between grocery and living quarters by a simple canvas curtain draped across the middle of the room. Ma Bender would cook meals, and sister Kate would serve them.

The Benders, meanwhile, attended church with their neighbors, and the young adults were seen as quite outgoing.

Ma and Pa didn't speak much, but locals described Kate as a vivacious spiritualist who held men entranced with her beauty. Kate even worked for a time as a waitress at the Cherryvale Hotel. She promoted herself all over the neighboring counties as a healer, which was not uncommon in those days. Some travelers and fellow churchgoers were standoffish about her palm reading and numerology practices, finding them wicked and abominable. John Jr. was agreeable enough, but often giggled when he spoke, giving off the impression that he was "simple," in the lingo of that era.

Many men who traveled alone would spend the night here, sleeping on a simple straw mattress on the floor, and they were often spellbound by Kate Bender's claims of psychic and healing abilities. The house was a welcome refuge to travelers wary of highway bandits, Native Americans or severe weather, so it's understandable why it would be an appealing stop for anyone. Over time, though, travelers coming through the area began to mysteriously disappear.

In May 1871, a stonemason named William Jones was discovered in nearby Drum Creek with his throat cut and his skull smashed in. He had been on his way to Independence with cash on hand for a land claim. No suspects were found, though some suspected the owner of the claim had something to do with it. Then in February 1872, after the melting of snow from a large blizzard, the bodies of two men were discovered out on the

GOVERNOR'S PROCLAMATION.

$2,000 REWARD

State of Kansas, Executive Department.

WHEREAS, several atrocious murders have been recently committed in Labette County, Kansas, under circumstances which fasten, beyond doubt, the commissions of these crimes upon a family known as the "Bender family," consisting of

JOHN BENDER, about 60 years of age, five feet eight or nine inches in height, German, speaks but little English, dark complexion, no whiskers, and sparely built;

MRS. BENDER, about 50 years of age, rather heavy set, blue eyes, brown hair, German, speaks broken English;

JOHN BENDER, Jr., alias John Gebardt, five feet eight or nine inches in height, slightly built, gray eyes with brownish tint, brown hair, light moustache, no whiskers, about 27 years of age, speaks English with German accent;

KATE BENDER, about 24 years of age, dark hair and eyes, good looking, well formed, rather bold in appearance, fluent talker, speaks good English with very little German accent:

AND WHEREAS, said persons are at large and fugitives from justice, now therefore, I, Thomas A. Osborn, Governor of the State of Kansas, in pursuance of law, do hereby offer a **REWARD OF FIVE HUNDRED DOLLARS** for the apprehension and delivery to the Sheriff of Labette County, Kansas, of each of the persons above named.

In Testimony Whereof, I have hereunto subscribed my name, and caused the Great Seal of the State to be affixed.

[L. S.]   Done at Topeka, this 17th day of May, 1873.

THOMAS A. OSBORN,
Governor.

By the Governor:
W. H. SMALLWOOD,
Secretary of State.

Governor's proclamation for a $2,000 reward for capture of the Bender family, 1873. *Courtesy of Kansas Historical Society.*

prairie near Oswego. They were similarly cut ear to ear and had their skulls bashed in. They were never identified, as so many people traveled up and down the trail it was hard to keep track of everyone. Some people suspected that horse thieves had something to do with this, and vigilance committees were created to run suspicious characters out of the region.

Over time, there were more and more reports of disappearances along the trail. A young man named Johnny Boyle headed south on the trail from Osage Mission with nearly $2,000 in cash. He was never to be heard from again. Another traveling man, Ben Brown, disappeared with his wagon and two horses. Mrs. Leroy Dick, the local township officer's wife, had a visiting cousin, a young man in his twenties named Henry McKenzie, who was heading to Independence and disappeared with $2,000 on him as well. William F. McCrotty was carrying $2,600 in cash and was traveling from Osage Mission when he disappeared. There was even a widower named George Loncher who was setting out for Iowa with his young daughter to take her to live with her grandparents. Neither were heard from again after purchasing a wagon and team of horses from local doctor William York.

These disappearances didn't go unnoticed, though, as Mr. Leroy Dick received many letters and personal visits from relatives searching for loved ones who had never returned from simple day trips along that trail. In March 1873, William York disappeared while traveling to Fort Scott. York, unlike many of the other unfortunate dead and vanished, had two influential and powerful brothers who were determined to get answers as to his whereabouts. One brother, Alexander York, served as a Kansas state senator and had military experience as a former colonel in the Union army.

When Colonel York arrived in Labette County, he brought his brother, Edward York, and fifty to sixty men to comb the area along the trail. Interviewing merchants and townsfolk in every nearby town, they discovered that Dr. York was last seen in Parsons on March 10 and that a merchant advised him to stay at the Bender house if he was going to be on the road. Arriving at the Bender house, the family told Colonel York that the doctor had stayed there, then continued on his way the next day. Kate offered to go into a spiritual trance to get answers as to Dr. York's whereabouts, but the search party replied with skepticism and disinterest. York asked about a report of a woman who claimed the Benders threatened her with guns and knives before fleeing their inn, but Ma Bender denied it, describing the woman as "a witch, a bad

The pit of death under a trap door at the Bender House, 1873. *Courtesy of Kansas Historical Society.*

and wicked woman." The searchers visited them again the next day, eventually thinking that they are just simple people who had no hand in anything criminal.

For the next few weeks, there was no news, until April 29, when an abandoned wagon and horses were discovered by a river outside of town. The horses were hungry, having been tethered to the wagon for days, and had begun chewing on the wood of the wagon. Bullet holes and blood were found on the sides of the wagon as well, and a sign that said "groceries" sat in the bed. Days later, on May 1, a neighbor passing by the Bender house

The infamous Bender murder house, 1872. *Courtesy of Kansas Historical Society.*

noticed starving and neglected animals roaming about the property. He looked inside, and the place was emptied out and abandoned.

When word spread that the Benders had left without notifying anyone, Leroy Dick led a party of forty men to the property to investigate. Curious onlookers came throughout the day to view the investigation firsthand. Searching the house, the investigators noticed a rotting stench coming from under a trap door in the floor. Down in this cellar, they discovered blood splattered everywhere, but nothing else. Moving the house off its foundations, they dug under it and still found nothing. The earth in the garden, though, seemed to have been freshly turned. It was there that they found Dr. York with his head smashed in and his throat cut. Continuing the next day, they discovered nearly a dozen bodies (accounts differ) buried nearby. Among the dead were Ben Brown, William McCrotty, Johnny Boyle, Henry McKenzie, George Loncher and his young daughter, as well as the bodies of an unidentified woman and man. Nearly a thousand onlookers witnessed this macabre spectacle, with many of the excavators grieving as they pieced these crimes together.

Over time, and through interviews with people who stayed at the Bender house, the investigators came to a theory of how the Benders operated. Guests were implored to sit at the dining table with their back to the dividing curtain, and that's where they would be hit in the head from behind with a hammer wielded by either John Sr. or John Jr. Large hammers were found under the stove—some of these were likely the murder weapons. It may have been easier to distract the traveling men with Kate's seductive presence at the table asking them all about where they were going and what their business was. The body would then be dumped into the cellar, where the throat was slit, and the body could be searched for cash and other valuables. After dark, the bodies might be dumped on the prairie, dropped into a well or buried in the orchard behind the house.

A couple of travelers told identical stories about declining to sit with their backs to the curtain, which enraged Ma Bender. They each decided to leave after seeing the male Benders emerge from behind the curtain and getting a strange feeling about the whole situation. That decision about where to sit saved their lives.

The sensational discovery led to nationwide newspaper coverage, a large manhunt and a governor's reward of $2,000 and $1,000 from Senator York to anyone who could help the authorities apprehend the Benders. Station agents in Kansas City and Thayer claimed to have seen them. Other theories had them heading to west Texas, where settlements were spread out and the law was stretched thin. A few privately funded search parties looked there to no avail. Some people speculate that the foursome split up, with the men leaving the women somewhere, or the young leaving the old. A number of women suspected of being Ma or Kate were arrested, but nothing came of it.

Modern crime authors call them America's first serial-killing family, and the mysteries surrounding them have never failed to fascinate readers. In reality, nobody knows what happened to the Benders and possibly might never know. For every theory about the Benders, there are ten equally compelling and competing countertheories. Perhaps they weren't even named Bender, as there was no documented evidence of their identity. Brother and sister might have actually been husband and wife playing a role. With such a deceitful group of people, there's no telling how deep their lies went and who they even really were.

John Wesley Hardin: Bullets in Bed

A lot of stories about the Wild West are exaggerated, and many tales of gunfights and outlaws were inflated by the participants themselves or misrepresented later by Hollywood. There are, however, a few individuals who were legitimately wild and ruthless. One of the most colorful, and easily annoyed, characters in that era was a Texan by the name of John Wesley Hardin. Hardin had no qualms about killing a man—especially if he snored.

Born in 1853 as the son of a Methodist preacher, Hardin fell far from his father's example and had many run-ins with the law from an early age. He also had a temper that was impossible to control. He was often in trouble at school and even once nearly stabbed a classmate to death during a fight. He said that he killed his first man at age fifteen. He challenged his uncle's former slave, Major Holshousen, to a wrestling match, and after defeating him, got into a fight with him the next day and shot him to death. Running from the law, he said that he killed three Union soldiers who were sent to apprehend him. His life as a fugitive had begun, and he was just a teenager.

Over the next few years, he was on the run and traveled with outlaw Frank Polk. He had several kills over card games, robberies, unpaid fees to pimps and petty disputes. Studying how to draw his guns the quickest, he sewed his holsters into his vest so that the butts of his pistols pointed inward. When he crossed his arms to draw, he could pull out both guns faster than anyone. He practiced his draw daily, which paid off in many instances. He claimed to have killed forty-two men over the course of his life. Newspaper accounts from that era attribute at least twenty-seven deaths to him, but the exact number is unclear. Though he was a master exaggerator, many of his stories are true.

After murdering a city marshal in Waco, Texas, in January 1871, he escaped and hit the Chisholm Trail as a cowboy to avoid prosecution. The eighteen-year-old could still not contain his rage and murdered a Mexican cowboy whose passing herd crowded into his. Arriving in Abilene in June, Hardin was confronted by none other than town marshal "Wild" Bill Hickok and was advised to avoid trouble. Hickok ordered him to hand over his guns, as they weren't allowed to be worn per city ordinance. Though Hickok didn't know anything about Hardin or his crimes, Hardin knew and respected Hickok. Hickok had a reputation as a formidable lawman, having killed several men himself in the preceding years. Because of this respect, Hardin handed over the guns without incident. This likely would not have happened with many other lawmen.

Later in the summer, Hardin was back in Abilene after another cattle drive and struck up a friendship with Wild Bill. He admired the old gunfighter and was something of a starstruck fan of his. Hickok saw himself in the young man and thought that maybe, with some growing up, the kid could eventually grow into a decent member of society. He heard stories of his past but was uninterested in prosecuting crimes that happened outside his jurisdiction. Hickok even let him carry his pistols in town now, and they womanized, drank whiskey and played cards together for several weeks.

Not long after, though, on August 6, Hardin got a room at the American House Hotel with his cousin Gip Clements and a rancher friend named Charles Couger. After a night of gambling and heavy drinking, they settled into their two rooms to sleep it off. Couger woke Hardin sometime during the night by snoring loudly in an adjacent room, and Hardin yelled through the wall for the man to "roll over." When the snoring continued, the drunk Hardin pulled out his revolver and fired several bullets through the wall to wake him up. Hearing no response, Hardin realized he might have shot too low. The first bullet missed, but the second hit Couger in the head, killing him instantly.

Likely not meaning to kill Couger, Hardin still knew he had broken a city ordinance by firing a gun inside city limits. Though he had struck up a friendship with Wild Bill, he knew this was not a forgivable act. He later stated, "I believed that if Wild Bill found me in a defenseless condition, he would take no explanation, but would kill me to add to his reputation." Hardin and Clements slipped out of the hotel that night from a second-story window. They landed on a lower roof and scrambled down to the ground. When Hardin saw Hickok arrive with four other policemen, he escaped and hid in a haystack for the remainder of the night. Stealing a horse in the morning, he headed back to Texas, never returning to Abilene.

Hardin continued to live the life of an outlaw and was eventually captured after the murder of Brown County, Texas's popular sheriff deputy Charles Webb and served fifteen years in the Huntsville, Texas state penitentiary. He tried to go straight but was shot to death in 1895 by an El Paso policeman who was looking to establish his own reputation as a gunman. Hardin committed many crimes but is mostly remembered today as a man "so mean, he once shot a man for snoring." He would later refer to this episode, saying, "They tell lots of lies about me. They say I killed six or seven men for snoring. Well, it ain't true. I only killed one man for snoring."

Gunfight at Hide Park

In the history of legendary stories of Wild West shootouts, one often thinks of the gunfight at the O.K. Corral—the infamous 1881 battle in Tombstone, Arizona, between lawmen and a group of outlaws. This shootout, which lasted thirty seconds, resulted in three dead and involved such famous lawmen as Wyatt Earp and Doc Holliday. It has led to many books, movies and other media depictions. One might also think of the 1892 shootout in Coffeyville, Kansas, in which all four Dalton Gang members were killed by townspeople after the gang tried to rob two banks at once in broad daylight.

There's another battle that took place on August 19, 1871, in Newton, Kansas, that was just as bloody. History, though, is selective with what stories are chosen for infamy. This battle involved no famous gunfighters or lawmen, and its result didn't catapult anyone to fame because the most important participant simply walked away and disappeared forever.

Newton got its start like many towns of its era, when the Atchison, Topeka and Santa Fe Railroad established a terminal there during the heyday of the cattle drives. Situated north of Wichita and south of rowdy Abilene, Newton soon became a center of activity and commerce for cowboys traveling north from Texas. Cattle had previously been brought to Abilene, but Newton was quickly taking the mantle as the terminus of the Chisholm Trail. With its growth came the entertainment and vices that naturally arose with the influx of cowboys: inns, gambling halls and saloons. Twenty-seven saloons and eight gambling halls, as well as a few inns, flophouses and brothels, were established in a short time. Trouble soon followed, as it always does with a large influx of men and a thin law enforcement presence. One newspaper writer of the era said, "I have been in a good many towns, but Newton is the fastest one I have ever seen. Here you may see young girls not over sixteen drinking whisky, smoking cigars, cursing and swearing until one almost loses the respect they should have for the weaker sex. The men are no better."

This incident, though, had its start with an argument between two lawmen who were hired to work together. These lawmen, Texas cowboy Billy Bailey and Irish Ohioan transplant Mike McCluskie, had a number of political disagreements that escalated into arguments. Being that they were hired as special policemen to keep order during new elections, their growing animosity became highly ironic. On August 11, 1871, a heated Election Day debate erupted between them at the Red Front Saloon in downtown Newton. This argument progressed into a fist fight, and McCluskie knocked Bailey out of the saloon and into the street. While Bailey was recovering, McCluskie stepped outside and drew his pistol, firing two shots at him. One hit him in the chest. Bailey lasted until the next day and died on August 12.

McCluskie immediately skipped town to avoid arrest but returned a few days later after hearing from friends that the incident would likely be deemed self-defense. The fact that Bailey had previously killed two men in three different gunfights was going to be McCluskie's excuse, even though Bailey didn't even pull his weapon on him. Telling many people that he feared for his life, McCluskie was comfortable enough to stay in Newton.

Several of Bailey's fellow Texan cowboys were in town though, and they knew McCluskie was back. They kept an eye out for his movements, vowing revenge. Just eight days after the killing, on August 19, McCluskie went to gamble at an area of town called Hide Park, which was likely thus dubbed because the ladies there "showed their hides," as cowboys said. Settling into a chair at a faro (card game) table at Tuttles Dance Hall, McCluskie was accompanied by his friend, Jim Martin. Three cowboys—Billy Garrett, Henry Kearns and Jim Wilkerson—entered the saloon around two o'clock in the morning. All were friends of Bailey, and Garrett had even killed two men himself in previous gunfights. Along with these three men, another man, a wealthy Texas rancher's son named Hugh Anderson, showed up. He yelled at McCluskie, "You are a cowardly son of a bitch! I will blow the top of your head off!"

With this escalation of tensions and the four men standing over them, Jim Martin stood up and pleaded with the men to stand down and to avoid a fight. Ignoring Martin, Hugh Anderson pulled his pistol and shot McCluskie in the neck, sending him to the floor. McCluskie grabbed his gun and tried to shoot Anderson back, but his gun misfired. Anderson stood over him and finished him off with several shots in the back. The other three men, Kearns, Wilkerson and Garrett, began firing as well to ward off the crowd, and one hit McCluskie as well. Their vengeful execution had been successful, and they prepared to leave the establishment.

Little did they realize that there was a young man in the saloon named James Riley. He was an eighteen-year-old who had recently been taken in by McCluskie and was referred to by many as "McCluskie's shadow." Riley was dying of tuberculosis and had never been involved in any kind of fight or gun battle before, but he did own two loaded Colt revolvers that he carried with him. In the smoke and low visibility of the room from all of the recent gunfire, Riley opened fire on the men with his two guns.

Kearns, Garrett and a bystander, railroad employee Patrick Lee, were all killed in the hail of bullets. Garrett was hit in the shoulder and chest and died a few hours later, while Kearns lingered for a week before his death. Lee was hit in the stomach and died two days later. Another railroad employee was shot in the calf, but he recovered. Everyone but Anderson was out of ammunition, and Wilkerson, Anderson and another bystander were wounded. Wilkerson was hit in the nose and leg and Anderson took two shots in the leg, but both recovered. Jim Martin, McCluskie's friend and would-be peacemaker, was hit in the neck and stumbled out of the saloon. He died across the street on the steps of Krum's Dance Hall. Some accounts claim that Riley locked the saloon doors so no one could escape, but it doesn't seem very likely, as he might not have had the time.

Once his guns were empty, and with seven men lying on the floor, Riley walked away from the stunned room and simply left town, never to be heard from again. Some locals think that he assumed a new name and started a new life elsewhere; however, his tuberculosis makes that scenario unlikely. He likely died shortly afterward. Townsfolk were horrified at the carnage, with one eyewitness telling the *Emporia News*,

> *It seems that this murderous affair was the result of several less fatal shooting scrapes, which have been happening at Newton for some weeks. It must be borne in mind that the state of society in that town is now at its worst. The town is largely inhabited by prostitutes, gamblers and whisky-sellers. Pistol shooting is the common amusement. All the frequenters of the saloons, gambling dens and houses of ill-fame are armed at all times, mostly with two pistols.*

Anderson, McCluskie's killer, was smuggled out of town by friends and put on a train to Texas, where he recovered from his wounds. A warrant was issued for his arrest, but he was never brought to trial for the murder. There's a tall tale that Mike McCluskie's brother, Arthur, vowed revenge and got his chance in 1873 when Anderson returned to Kansas to work as a bartender at a place in Medicine Lodge called Harding's Trading Post. As the story goes, on July 4, 1873, one of Arthur's friends invited Anderson to a duel with either guns or knives. Choosing guns, both men emerged from the trading post and prepared for the showdown. After both men fired numerous shots at each other, they pulled knifes, and both died in the ensuing struggle. This tale was almost certainly fabricated and was denied by many Kansas newspapers after the *New York World* ran a fantastical story about it.

With five killed and multiple others wounded, this gunfight made a lot of noise in the press. The *Lawrence Journal-World* called it a "riot." The *Emporia News* called it "wholesale murder at Newton," and Topeka's *Kansas Daily Commonwealth* dubbed it "butchery." It has largely been forgotten by history, and there are no historical markers of this infamous event. The town of Newton was justifiably horrified and didn't want to memorialize it. Hide Park was removed and is now a row of homes in the 200 block of West Second

Street. No original structures remain, and citizens of Harvey County were all too happy to rid themselves of the cowboy element after the railhead moved out of town. Twelve killings were reported during the 1871 cattle season, and by the next year the town passed a law prohibiting the running of cattle through town. With the railroad line extended to Wichita, the "wickedest city in the west" could fade into history. This massacre, though, led to many gun-surrender laws in towns across the West (as in Abilene), and the carrying of firearms was increasingly limited for public safety.

The Nicest Boy in Wolcott

On November 28, 1958, eighteen-year-old University of Kansas sophomore Lowell Lee Andrews was home for Thanksgiving break in Wolcott, Kansas—a small town near Kansas City—with his parents, William and Opal, and his sister, Jennie Marie. His twenty-year-old sister was home from college in Oklahoma. As the rest of the family watched television in the darkened living room downstairs, Lowell was upstairs reading the final chapter of Dostoevsky's *The Brothers Karamazov*. Around seven that night, he shaved, put on his finest suit and loaded two .22 caliber guns—a Luger pistol and a rifle—from a closet. Holstering the pistol at his hip, he marched downstairs with the rifle slung across his chest.

Without warning, Lowell switched on the living room light, pointed the rifle at his sister and fired, hitting her right between the eyes and killing her instantly. He then fired six shots at his mother and two at his father. Though his mother died instantly, his father did not succumb, and he crawled across the floor to the kitchen. Lowell calmly followed him and emptied the pistol into him. He reloaded twice and hit him seventeen times in all. This brutal massacre had been carried out by a boy who one neighbor lady called "the nicest boy in Wolcott."

Andrews was a highly intelligent, bookish boy who many around the small town of Wolcott considered to be extremely polite. A big kid, more than six feet tall and 260 pounds, he lacked social skills and preferred spending his evenings alone in his room with his books. He was a regular church-going Baptist—members of the congregation described him as "sweet and gentle"—and his parents operated a successful farm. His mother often worried that he should be more social but figured that his shyness and reservation was due to his being heavyset at this awkward teenage phase of his life.

In high school, Lowell showed a talent for music and science, and after he graduated in 1957, he enrolled at the University of Kansas in Lawrence, an hour's drive from home. Playing bassoon in the university orchestra and studying zoology, he seemed to be branching out and adjusting well. He mostly kept to himself and was a model student. Classmates and professors at the university recalled him as "gentle and sweet natured." Little did anyone know that he had a delusional fantasy: killing his parents to get an inheritance so he could lead the life of a gangster in Chicago.

William and Opal Andrews owned land worth more than $200,000 and were well regarded by their neighbors and fellow churchgoers. They were active members of the Grandview Baptist Church, which was led by minister Virto Dameron. Expecting to inherit the 240-acre farm and $1,850 in savings, Lowell saw himself living a glamorous new life as a mafia hit man. He intended to drive expensive cars, dress well and carry out killings for hire in this exciting fantasy he had concocted. He considered poisoning the family for a while but eventually settled on this more dramatic option.

That night, after the killings, Andrews went around the house disturbing the drawers, furniture and everyone's belongings to make it look like a robbery. He also raised his bedroom window, removed the screen and scattered the contents of his room. He then drove the forty miles of snowy and icy roads back to his college town of Lawrence, where he threw his now-disassembled weapons off the Massachusetts Street bridge into the Kansas River. Stopping by his boardinghouse, he chatted with his landlady and told her that he had dropped by to get his typewriter for a homework assignment. Lastly, he went downtown to the Granada Theater and took in a late showing of the film *Mardi Gras*, starring Pat Boone. A candy counter girl and an usher described him as "unusually talkative."

After the movie ended at eleven o'clock, he made his way back to Wolcott with his alibi established. Pulling in around midnight, he fed the family dog and then called the sheriff to report a robbery. The first deputy on the scene, a man named Myers, described what happened next: "This big, dark-haired boy, Lowell Lee, he was sitting on the porch petting his dog. Lieutenant Athey asked the boy what happened, and he pointed to the door, real casual, and said, 'Look in there.'"

Andrews seemed so nonchalant about his entire family being murdered that they questioned him repeatedly about his whereabouts and actions that night. Another officer asked him about funeral arrangements, and his suspicions went through the roof when Andrews replied, "I don't care what you do with them."

Around three o'clock in the morning, the sheriff woke the family minister, Mr. Dameron, and convinced him to come have a talk with Lowell. At the jail, Dameron shared a Coca-Cola with Lowell and asked him about Thanksgiving and his second year of college. He then went straight to the question, "You didn't do this terrible thing, did you? If you did, now is the time to purge your soul." Andrews nodded and confessed right there.

Feeling no remorse and remarking that he "didn't feel anything about it," he calmly said exactly what was on his mind, "The time came, and I was doing what I had to do. That's all there is to it. I am not sorry, and I am not glad. I have no feeling." He was stone-faced when he guided police divers to the spot in the river where he dumped the murder weapons.

Andrews was taken to the Menninger Clinic in Topeka—a leading center of psychotherapy research—where Dr. Joseph Satten deemed him to be schizophrenic, though not delusional. Satten had been studying a type of murder that he called "sudden murders" in which the killer appears sane before and after the crime but barely has a logical motive. Though Andrews knew that he committed the crime, and though he knew by the law that he deserved punishment, he felt nothing either way about the murders. His lawyer's insanity defense failed at trial, and he was sentenced to hang, as Kansas still had the death penalty at the time. Requests for clemency from the governor of Kansas and appeals to the U.S. Supreme Court were denied. The appeal had previous legal precedent and might have actually worked. In one famous case in state history, sixteen-year-old John Kornstett murdered his ten-year-old cousin in 1901 and was sent to death row. He was released a decade later upon appeal to the governor.

Sent to death row at Lansing Prison, he would later share space with infamous *In Cold Blood* killers Dick Hickock and Perry Smith. Smith was annoyed by him, as Andrews would always correct his grammar. Hickock got a kick out of him, and Truman Capote recalled him saying that "Andy was a funny kid. It was like I told him, he had no respect for human life, not even his own." Each of these men faced death row in a different way. Smith hated the authorities and attempted to starve himself to deny their power to kill him. Hickock accepted the sentence but never gave up on schemes to free himself through appeals to the Kansas Bar Association. Andrews was absolutely complacent and told the others, "Sooner or later

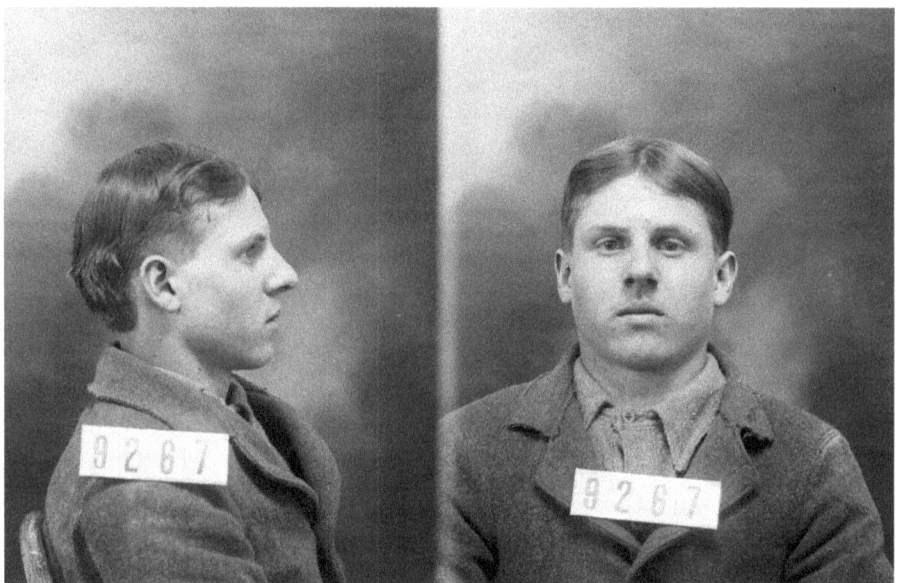

Murderer John Kornstett, 1901. *Courtesy of Kansas Historical Society.*

we'll all get out of here. Either walk out—or be carried out in a coffin. Myself, I don't care whether I walk or get carried."

Andrews was scheduled to hang on November 30, 1962, and ate his last meal of fried chicken, mashed potatoes, green beans and pie à la mode before his final walk. Reporters on the scene said that he declined any last words and seemed "outwardly remorseless and disinterested." In one of his final acts before he died, he gave Hickock a few lines from a Thomas Gray poem. The last line read, "The paths of glory lead but to the grave." Interestingly enough, after his hanging, he was buried next to his parents and sister at Mount Salem Cemetery in his mother's hometown of Excello, Missouri.

Andrews is mentioned in several pages of Capote's *In Cold Blood*. He has also been portrayed in three films: Bowman Upchurch played him in the original adaptation of *In Cold Blood*, C. Ernst Harth played him in *Capote* and Ray Gestaut played him in *Infamous*. He has often been seen as a footnote in the Capote story, but his own story is arguably more chilling than Capote's in the sense that he did this to his own family and not to some unfortunate strangers.

Rufus King: The Stable Owner With a Heinous Double Life

Maple Hill is a small community of just more than six hundred citizens, roughly thirty minutes west of Topeka. Founded in 1882, the town has always been close knit, and the historic population didn't rise above three hundred until the 1970s. Since it was such a modest agricultural community, most of the excitement anyone experienced involved going into Topeka or Kansas City. Most community gatherings involved church or school events, and a predictable slow pace governed their daily lives.

That all changed one day in August 1919, when some children were playing in sheds around an old livery stable. They found a tattered old gunny sack hanging in one of the sheds and looked inside…and found a human skeleton.

The children rushed home and promptly reported the find to their parents, who in turn were horrified and notified the county sheriff. Everyone in town knew that local man Rufus King owned the livery stable, and he quickly became suspect number one. He was in Colorado working for a construction company when the investigation started. King had a reputation around town as an intimidating, sullen, mean character, and when people started suspecting him, stories of missing men began to resurface. Townsfolk mostly described him as a married Spanish-American War veteran with a dark temper.

In the meantime, the bones and smashed skull from the sack were identified as Reuben Gutshall of Rossville, a town just eight miles away. Gutshall had been missing since December 1913, and it was known that King was the last person to see him because the boy worked for him. King had told Gutshall's family, and others who were searching for Gutshall, that he had gotten into a troubled situation with a girl and left town. The day after his disappearance, King was using Gutshall's wagon and team of horses, claiming he had bought them. Even more brazen, King showed up at the Gutshall home a day or two later and loaded up some of the missing boy's possessions as well as eighty bushels of corn, claiming that he had paid $160 for it all.

Reuben Gutshall's brother, John, was the one who identified the bones, noting the jawbone, height and other marks were consistent with medical statements about the youth. A complaint charging King with murder was issued, and from here, the investigation went into full force and a sensation ensued.

According to the August 21, 1919 edition of the *Alma Signal*, "Thousands of curiosity seekers packed the little town of Maple Hill Sunday afternoon" to witness the search for more bodies. The article went on to describe the scene: "Hundreds of motor cars from every city and town within a radius of fifty miles began arriving in Maple Hill in the early morning. By noon, out of town cars filled every available parking spot on the main streets."

In the era before such distractions as the internet, television and social media, an event like this could accurately be described as a macabre "happening." The owner of the local hardware store opened his shop and distributed new digging tools to almost one hundred volunteer searchers. The authorities directed teams of these volunteer men to systematically dig trenches across the livery stable property. One searcher punched a long, sharp-pointed iron prod into the ground at random and struck a hard object in the earth under an old manure pile. The huge crowd formed and shoved around him as the workers unearthed a pelvis.

Kansas assistant attorney general Maurice McNeill directed the digging squad to carefully remove the dirt around the bones. The body lay face down with a "rotten shirt clinging to his shoulder blades." The hair, still attached to the skull, was straight and black. The authorities brought up local man, James Woody, to see if he could identify the skull. His son, John, had been missing since 1909, and the last person to see him alive was none other than Rufus King.

Ten years earlier, John was a twenty-year-old man who had saved money to purchase his own horses and a buggy. One day, he simply disappeared, and when his family inquired as to his whereabouts, Rufus King told them that John had sold him his horse and buggy and had taken the money to move to Oklahoma. He told the parents that Woody even sent him a letter, but he failed to produce it. He gave them an address where they could get in touch with him, but their letter returned undeliverable. For ten agonizing years, John's parents worried about him and wondered why he had not contacted them. The story Rufus King told them didn't quite sit well with them, but they never proposed an investigation because they had nothing to really go on.

As James Woody crouched down into this shallow six-inch-deep grave, he inspected the bones and immediately recognized them as his son because John had two gold fillings on the sides of his two front teeth. James turned to McNeill and stated, "There is not a doubt in my mind. This is the body of my son." James was one of the first volunteers to dig at the King place and was certain he would find his son there. According to some accounts, it was

Left: Serial killer Rufus King shown in his service uniform during the Spanish-American War. *Courtesy of Kansas Historical Society.*

Right: John Anderson Woody, victim of Rufus King. Photo taken between 1905–9. *Courtesy of Kansas Historical Society.*

presumed that John was choked to death in his sleep at the livery stable after playing poker late into the night.

Roughly thirty feet away, diggers discovered another skeleton on the property. This one was the body of a middle-aged jewelry peddler who was traveling through the county. His skull had been smashed in, similar to Gutshall's, and he was buried with the barrel of a .22 rifle. The authorities suspected that the killer used the barrel of the rifle or another similar implement to smash the skulls in. The jewelry peddler, who had suddenly disappeared years ago, was wrapped in a horse blanket and had a rope tied around his neck. Found with the body was a cuff link made from a shell similar to some that King had in his possession.

Once the media took hold of this story, several people from surrounding states started inquiring to the local authorities about missing loved ones and the possibility that there were more bodies in Maple Hill. One such missing person, Fred Williams, was a wealthy landowner from Versailles, Missouri, who disappeared in 1912 on a land-buying trip to Wabaunsee County. His daughter wrote to the Kansas attorney general, saying he had a large amount of money on him and simply never returned after boarding a train in Tipton, Missouri. Nothing came of this lead, but there were many people who were suspicious that King had something to do with this disappearance as well.

King recognized the suspicion he was under and had by now brought his wife out to Pueblo, Colorado. Upon his arrest in Colorado, he was brought to Alma, the county seat of Wabaunsee County, just down the road from Maple Hill. The county sheriff, recognizing that passions were running high, feared that King would be lynched, and other deputies and marshals from across the county came to Alma to guard him. King was later removed to Topeka.

As soon as he could make it to Topeka, Assistant Attorney General McNeill went to the Shawnee County jail to interview King. When he arrived, he could hear King saying to his brother through the cell's bars, "If I have to pass over to the other side for these crimes they say I done, they'll know, on the other side, that I didn't have anything to do with it. I don't know how them bones come to be there. Things sure look bad for me." McNeill cross-examined King. He asked King how he knew the jewelry peddler, why he left Maple Hill and why Woody would leave for Oklahoma. King denied everything and stuck to his stories that these men left on their own volitions and sold their belongings to him.

King's preliminary trial was held in nearby Eskridge, but the public was so animated over the murders that he was moved to a jail in Lyndon. In Lyndon, in November 1920, it only took the jury twenty-nine minutes to reach a verdict of guilty in the case of the murder of John Woody, which was the most solid case. When the foreman, J.S. Oyler, prepared to pronounce the verdict, the "drop of a pin could be heard in the court room," according to the *Quenemo News*. As soon as he spoke the word "guilty," the audience burst into tremendous applause. He was subsequently found guilty of the other two murders as well. King grew pale but otherwise didn't react. Nearly eight hundred people were in the room, and the courthouse was so packed that the doors could not be closed. A balcony even had to be cleared of people in fear that it may collapse.

King was sentenced to life in prison, and he was sent to the Kansas State Penitentiary in Lansing. Before he went, he threatened vengeance against several people who spoke up against him. A native of Maple Hill who was a member of the Kansas legislature visited the penitentiary on official tours and said that each time he saw King, he would renew these threats to all those who had any part in his downfall. He never got the opportunity to act on them, though, as he died in prison still serving his sentence. King wasn't the first serial killer in Kansas state history, but he was the first one to be caught and sensationally brought to justice for his crimes.

Not the Least Bit Sorry

If there was a list of the most unrepentant criminals to grace the Sunflower State, Carl Panzram would be right at the top. His litany of crimes ran the entire gauntlet from petty burglaries, robberies and arson to rape, assault and serial killing. Continually being arrested and escaping from jails and prisons, his criminal career brought him to Kansas…and to his end.

Born in East Grand Forks, Minnesota, on June 28, 1892, Panzram said that by the age of five or six, he had already become a practiced liar and developed a penchant for theft. Bouncing around numerous juvenile courts many times from ages seven to eleven for drunkenness and disorderly conduct, his problems were apparent very early in life. His parents sent him to the Minnesota State Training School, where he was beaten, tortured and raped by staff members. He hated the place so much that he burned it down on July 7, 1905. He ran away from home in 1906 and took to the rails to begin his life of crime.

After drunkenly enlisting in the U.S. Army at age fifteen, he was convicted of larceny and sent to Leavenworth, Kansas, for his first prison sentence from 1908 to 1910. William Howard Taft, the future president and current secretary of war, approved his sentence. Panzram said that Leavenworth was the place that killed any goodness that was left in him and that his time in Kansas sent him into darkness. Leavenworth was the first prison with such a high level of professional security that it was near impossible to escape. No wonder he wanted out of Kansas as soon as possible. After his release, he lapsed right back into his old life.

After being dishonorably discharged from the army, he quickly ran afoul of the law and was arrested multiple times for theft across many states, including California, Texas, Idaho, Montana, Oregon, Connecticut, New York and Washington, D.C. He would steal anything from anyone, including cars, money, bicycles and even a yacht. He would also rape the men he robbed, showing a sadistic side that was emerging. He was often beaten for assaulting officers as well.

He claimed to have killed his first man in 1910 in Texas. He then stole thirty-five dollars from him. Using many aliases, he traveled from state to state stealing and reselling items. He helped a man murder a prison warden in Oregon, sawed through the bars in his cell and even had a dramatic shootout to escape.

In 1920, his killing spree began. He burglarized William Howard Taft's home in 1920 as revenge for his imprisonment in Kansas and even stole Taft's .45 caliber handgun. With the cash he stole from Taft, he bought a boat and lured sailors away from New York City bars. He robbed and raped them, then killed them with Taft's gun and threw their bodies overboard in Long Island Sound. He said he did this to ten men. He also took a trip to Africa, where he claimed to have killed a boy and then hired a boat with rowers, killed them and fed them to crocodiles.

With so many aliases and continual movement, he got away with more rapes, robberies and murders on the East Coast. In 1928, he was finally arrested for robbery in Baltimore, Maryland, and confessed to a few other crimes and murders. He received a sentence of twenty-five years to life due to his numerous crimes and admissions. He later wrote that he also wished to poison a city's water supply or sink a British ship in New York Harbor to start a war between England and America.

To his ultimate dismay, he returned to Leavenworth, which put him in such a dark mood that he warned the warden that he would "kill the first man that bothers me." Being very displeased to be back in Kansas, he began working on assignment alone in the prison's laundry room. On June 20, 1929, he took an iron bar and beat prison laundry foreman Robert Warnke to death. This was the final straw, and the State of Kansas sentenced him to death. There would be no more escapes, no more name changes, no more crimes.

There were many groups and individuals opposed to the death penalty who offered to help him appeal his sentence. He refused any appeals and wrote to such high-minded people that, "The only thanks you and your kind will ever get from me for your efforts on my behalf is that I wish you all had one neck and that I had my hands on it." One officer befriended him and gave him money for cigarettes and encouraged him to write. Panzram wrote that he had murdered twenty-one people; raped more than one thousand men; and committed hundreds of acts of burglary, arson and other crimes. He ended his tome with the line, "For all these things I am not the least bit sorry."

On September 5, 1930, Panzram impatiently walked to the gallows at Leavenworth and wanted to get on with it. When the officers were covering his head with the hood, he spat in the executioner's face. When they asked him if he had any last words, he characteristically retorted, "Yes, hurry it up, you Hoosier bastard! I could kill a dozen men while you're screwing around!" After his execution, he was buried under a simple prison gravestone inscribed 31614—his prisoner number. His was one of Kansas's most famous executions, with the state sending its final man to hang in 1965.

Panzram's murderous rage and total lack of remorse was studied in depth by famed Kansas psychologist and researcher Karl Menninger, who wrote about him in his book, *Man Against Himself*. How fitting that a great healer from Kansas would study the mind of a great destroyer who was finally stopped here for good. Menninger argued that psychiatric treatment could be used to help prevent individuals from committing crimes, and he advocated treating offenders like the mentally ill.

Thomas J. Smith: A Martyr For Law and Order

In the 1870s, Abilene, Kansas, grew into a rough-and-tumble cow town that had many of the trappings of the classic Wild West. It had saloons, prostitutes, drinking and occasional lawlessness. With the influx of cowboys from Texas, the need for law and order became apparent. One brave lawman stepped up to tame the town and paid with his life.

Abilene owes its growth as a cow town to Joseph McCoy. In the 1860s, Texas ranchers had many obstacles to getting their cattle to market because many homesteaders in Kansas didn't want these tick-laden cattle crossing their lands, as the "Texas fever" disease they often spread could affect Kansas livestock. With the Chisholm Trail established farther west than most settlements in the state at that time, the cattle could use it to travel north without too much interference. The railroads were also expanding westward and looking to increase revenues. It was the perfect opportunity for Mr. McCoy to step in and establish Abilene at the end of the trail, complete with a hotel, bank and stockyard, as well as other amenities near the Kansas Pacific Railway line. Once the cattle got there from Texas, they could be shipped by rail to Kansas City, Chicago and other cities in the East.

McCoy advertised his settlement all over Texas, and by 1870, thousands of cattle were making the trek northward. He had a modest goal of 200,000 cattle coming north in the next decade but far exceeded that when he brought more than 2 million cattle in just four years. In 1871, there were days when more than five thousand cowboys were being paid for their cattle in one day. The phrase "it's the Real McCoy" was born of this success, and the town's transient population exploded at this time.

After a long, hard cattle drive across hundreds of miles, and with money in their pockets, the well-paid cowboys found many ways to cause trouble on their well-earned vacation from the rough trail. Saloons, prostitution, gunfights and a general rowdiness challenged the fledgling authorities to step in and establish order. After three months of strict discipline on the trail, cowboys were ready to blow off some steam. After getting paid, they would often get a haircut, a wash and a new set of clothes, then hit the town. Drinking and gambling went hand in hand with fistfights and the occasional shootout.

Thomas J. Smith, chief of police in Abilene, 1870. *Courtesy of Kansas Historical Society.*

Abilene mayor Theodore Henry had a difficult time finding anyone willing to deal with them. A few local volunteers had attempted to act as lawmen but gave up. Two St. Louis policemen were hired but quit the same day that they arrived. One applicant, Thomas J. Smith, was on Henry's radar, and the mayor telegraphed for him to come out from Colorado and interview for the job. He had built a reputation as a brave lawman in Kit Carson, Colorado. Though he was five foot eleven and 170 pounds, which was a decent size for that era, Smith didn't overly impress Mayor Henry. The task was a big one and needed a firm character to stand up to it. Being described as a handsome man with a thick mustache, Smith's presence often commanded respect.

At forty years old, Smith allegedly served as a policeman in New York City and later as a marshal in Wyoming. When he served as marshal, a local vigilante group had lynched a railroad employee suspected of murder. A group of other railroad employees retaliated. Skirmishes erupted between the sides and nearly burned the entire town of Bear River City, Wyoming, to the ground. Smith had to keep both sides apart for several days until troops arrived from nearby Fort Bridger and imposed martial law. This event earned him the nickname Tom "Bear River" Smith.

Though Henry wasn't sure about Smith, he was hired as Abilene's first marshal on June 4, 1870, with a monthly wage of $150. Should a situation arise, he was expected to keep order by himself and with whomever he could deputize.

The first order of business for Smith was enforcing the city ordinance that prohibited the carrying of guns in town. This had been openly ignored by many cowboys, and the citizens of the town admired his lack of hesitation on this front. With this law, every person entering Abilene was required to check in their gun with the proprietor of their hotel. Smith himself almost never used his firearm, preferring his fists. As a boxer in his early years, he had a mean punch. He even disarmed two gun-toting characters named "Big Hank" Hawkins and "Wyoming Frank" during a fistfight. Afterward, he banished them from the town, causing a sensation, which led to the immediate respect of the citizenry and the mayor. In August, he successfully pursued some horse thieves to Nebraska and was given a raise of $225 a month. In September, he moved to close down the red-light district, which was full of "vile characters" in his mind. There were two assassination attempts on his life, but he continued on the job despite his high unpopularity with the cowboys.

On November 2, 1870, Smith deputized a local man, James McDonald, to help him serve a warrant for the arrest of anyone associated with the murder of an Abilene man named John Shea. Shea had supposedly been driving his small local herd of cattle across his neighbor's land when an argument broke out, resulting in his death. Two local farmers, Moses Miles and Andrew McConnell, were suspects, and Smith located them at a small dugout nearly ten miles outside of Abilene. After a brief gunfight, Smith was hit in the chest, and his deputy fled. Shooting back, he wounded McConnell, and a hand-to-hand struggle ensued. Miles incapacitated him when he hit him in the head with the butt of his rifle. He then took an axe and decapitated Smith in a grisly conclusion to the fight. The marshal had done his duty to the very end. It is a bit ironic that Smith came to town to clean up the habits of the unruly cowboys, only to be murdered by local farmers.

Returning to Abilene, McDonald raised a posse to get help, and upon arriving at the dugout, he discovered Smith dead. McConnell and Miles were apprehended three days later and were given twelve- and sixteen-year prison sentences, respectively. These lenient sentences are quite incredible considering the era of vigilante justice and the brutality of the murder. Their claim was that the lawmen didn't show any warrant or prove their authority. McDonald carried on in law enforcement through the next year, though a replacement was needed for Smith. He was replaced as marshal by none other than legendary gunfighter "Wild

Bill" Hickok in April 1871. Despite Hickok's fame, he never lived up to Smith's valiance as marshal. The town's rowdiness settled over time as railroads extended to Newton, Ellsworth and Wichita, making them more attractive destinations for cowboys.

Buried in Abilene with great ceremony, Smith was honored with a large tombstone and plaque detailing his sacrifice. On May 30, 1904, he was exhumed and given a new burial in a more prominent place at Abilene's north cemetery. A massive red granite rock weighing more than two tons was shipped from Oklahoma. Inscribed on the plaque are the simple words:

> *THOMAS J. SMITH*
> *Marshal of Abilene, 1870*
> *Died, a Martyr to Duty, Nov. 2, 1870*
> *A Fearless Hero of Frontier Days*
> *Who in Cowboy Chaos*
> *Established the Supremacy of Law*

United States president Dwight Eisenhower grew up in Abilene and considered Smith to be a personal hero, having visited his grave on many occasions—and three times while he was president. He held him in higher regard than Hickok and said of Smith, "According to the legends of my hometown, he was anything but dull. While he almost never carried a pistol, he…subdued the lawless by the force of his personality and his tremendous capacity as an athlete. One blow of his fist was apparently enough to knock out the ordinary 'tough' cowboy. He was murdered by treachery."

Ike wasn't the only U.S. president with a connection to Smith, though. United States president Ronald Reagan portrayed Smith in one of his final acting roles in the 1965 episode "No Gun behind His Badge" of the television series *Death Valley Days*. Though Smith served only a few months as marshal before his untimely end, he set an example that is remembered to this day.

2
SECRET LIVES

THE ELLINWOOD MAN CAVES

Hopping off a train in the late nineteenth-century in the central Kansas town of Ellinwood, a man might survey the small town and see a few familiar sights. There were hotels, mercantile stores, druggists, churches and homes, just like any other town. There would be horses at hitching posts and men, women and children going about their daily lives. But to find a special place reserved for men, where he could have a drink, take a bath, get a haircut and be entertained by ladies of the night, he would need to go underground…literally.

Ellinwood lies along the old Santa Fe Trail, which saw heavy traffic across Kansas from the 1820s to the 1880s. With the founding of Barton County in 1867 and the changing fortunes of the booming cattle trails, Ellinwood was founded in 1871. Some cattle came through this area on their way north to Ellsworth, but it was only a fraction of what went to Abilene.

This all changed in 1872 when the City of Abilene banned cowboys due to the destruction of the land from the massive herds, the tick fever they brought from Texas and the general lawlessness of the cowboys themselves. Now there was an opportunity for another town to take Abilene's place, and the citizens of Ellsworth, about sixty miles west of Abilene, encouraged drovers to march their herds to their town. This new offshoot of the trail west of the original terminus brought cattle north across the Arkansas River right at Ellinwood. The number of Texas longhorns jumped from 30,000 to 220,000 in one year. This new offshoot of the trail was sometimes referred to as "Cox's Trial," "The Ellsworth Trail" and—least creatively—the "Middle Branch of the Chisholm Trial."

With the arrival of the Santa Fe Railroad in 1872, the town was named after railroad engineer Colonel John R. Ellinwood. Because many German immigrants settled in central Kansas, the town's streets were given German names to entice them to settle there. You can find streets named "Wilhelm," "Goethe" and "Bismark" there. With the growth of the town as a busy stop for many travelers, a peculiar set of businesses also grew underneath the downtown.

Like many towns and cities of the late nineteenth century, Ellinwood boasted a system of tunnels connecting businesses underneath their downtown. Exact dates are hard to pin down because many tunnels were built and expanded as buildings were constructed, but it is likely that the large influx of German settlers after 1878 might have spurred the growth. With the town boasting a population of just 352 in 1880 and 760 by 1900, it's clear that the tunnels didn't have a large local population to serve, but they were very busy with travelers.

Originally running down each side of Main Street for two blocks, this underground world could be accessed by stairs in several places and was connected to a public bathhouse, shoe shop, barbershop and even a meat storage business. One such entrance lies under the Wolf Hotel, which sits right across from the Atchison, Topeka and Santa Fe Railroad Depot and was a perfect entry point for travelers. To access the tunnels, one would simply walk down creaky wooden steps into a gas lamp–lit world. Like the buildings above, the walls were fortified with native limestone and wood.

Since Ellinwood was a traditional, religious community, activities like prostitution, drinking and gambling could not be tolerated out in the open, so these vices thrived in these underground establishments. Women were not allowed down there unless they were prostitutes. Such women were dubbed "soiled doves." The men could get a lye soap bath for fifteen cents and hire a woman for twenty-five cents or more, depending on the lady.

A few other Kansas communities had similar underground tunnels and establishments hidden away from the world. You could find them in Fort Scott, Ellsworth, Leavenworth, Lincoln, Caldwell and Douglass. There are rumors of others that have been forgotten, as well. Kansas was not unique, and many other cities, such as Chicago and Indianapolis, had similar systems under their streets. You could even find bowling alleys in some of them, including in Ellsworth. The wooden sidewalks above them could be lifted to bring down supplies or to pour coal shipments. Larger cities needed the tunnels as conduits for bringing supplies to large downtown buildings—sometimes with literal underground trains—whereas smaller towns used them as a social refuge.

To understand the scale of this place, the underground had eleven saloons around the year 1900. They must have been crowded places full of card playing, music and drinking. There are stories of German residents retreating to the tunnels during World War I because of local anti-German sentiment. You can imagine that during Prohibition the tunnels would have had many other uses, especially as the German community had a deeply ingrained beer culture brought with them from overseas.

By the 1930s and 1940s, the tunnels had seen their heyday and had fallen into disuse and were closed off. In 1979 though, a woman named Adrianna Dierolf inherited some downtown property in Ellinwood and rediscovered this amazing hidden world. She gave tours for a few years, but the town put in new sidewalks in 1982 and filled most of the tunnels with sand. Adrianna was able to save a portion of the tunnels, including three of the businesses. They still last to this day, and tours take visitors down the narrow passageways and creaky steps. You can still see original flooring, wallpaper and a barber's chair from Jung's Barber Shop, as well as bathtubs, mirrors and other artifacts from that era. It just goes to show that even the smallest towns in Kansas had their vices…they just sometimes hid 'em away.

Breaking Bad on the Prairie

During the height of the Cold War at the tail end of the 1950s and early 1960s, the U.S. government built twenty-seven Atlas E missile silos across states such as Kansas, Washington and Wyoming to house Atlas Intercontinental Ballistic Missiles (ICBM). These large steel and concrete structures covered roughly twenty acres and had chain link fences around them to keep people out. Nine such complexes were built in eastern Kansas, all roughly within an hour and a half drive from 548th Strategic Missile Squadron's headquarters at Forbes Air Force Base in Topeka. Should a nuclear war with Russia commence, these ninety-foot-tall missiles could carry a four-megaton warhead six thousand miles to its target. After decommissioning, one was converted into a high school, some went into decay and one became the setting of the largest clandestine LSD laboratories in U.S. history.

One of the nine sites had been converted into a home in 1996 and was a curiosity to rural neighbors. Folks living nearby noticed vehicles coming and going, often at strange hours of the night and sometimes multiple times a night. The traffic was erratic. Some weeks there would be no one coming and going, and other weeks there would be consecutive nights of traffic. Neighbors in rural Kansas are often friendly and wave at each other as they drive by. The owners of this site, though, never waved and even locked the front gate, which struck many in this laid-back area as odd. People walking down the road would be told to leave.

It all made sense in November 2000, when the site was raided by law enforcement. Inside the secretive complex, Drug Enforcement Administration (DEA) agents discovered enough raw chemicals to make at least thirty-six million doses of LSD. They arrested two San Francisco natives, fifty-seven-year-old William Pickard and forty-seven-year-old Clyde Apperson. They were charged with conspiracy to manufacture and distribute LSD and were caught in possession of it as well. How had the authorities discovered all of this, though? As in many drug cases, it all boiled down to one paranoid partner losing his cool.

In 1996, a rich young man named Gordon Todd Skinner purchased the silo, which had been abandoned since its decommissioning in 1965. Skinner had extensive monetary resources from a large inherited fortune, and he had developed a passion for psychedelic drugs. He spent years converting the site into his own underground mansion, including the best televisions, hot tubs and sound systems. He even imported wood and marble. He told local officials that he was going to make the silo into a spring factory, which he did for a short time.

Skinner had ties to a California LSD manufacturer named William L. Pickard and convinced him to move his drug operation to the silo in Kansas. A lab partner, Clyde Apperson, came from California as well to assist Pickard. The DEA estimated that in the seclusion of the Kansas countryside, the pair produced nearly 90 percent of the LSD in America in the late 1990s. Skinner also made synthetic mescaline, which he manufactured despite having no training as a professional chemist.

Paranoia, as it often does in high-pressure situations involving criminal activities, got to Skinner and he informed the DEA of the operations. Pickard and Apperson were arrested while moving the laboratory out of the silo. Driving a rented Ryder truck and a Buick LeSabre, the pair were pulled over by the Kansas Highway Patrol instead of DEA vehicles in hopes that the pair wouldn't get suspicious. Sensing that something was up, Pickard bolted into nearby woods and authorities captured him the next day. Apperson went without incident.

Prosecutors at their subsequent trials based much of the case on testimony from Skinner, who had been granted immunity. Pickard and Apperson were described as well-connected underground chemists with a drug ring that had links to California and Europe. Witnesses verified that Pickard manufactured LSD in a movable lab at multiple locations, including Oregon, New Mexico, Colorado and Ellsworth County, Kansas. Pickard was shown to be no amateur, as he was once the deputy director of the Drug Policy Research Program at the University of California, Los Angeles. He also worked as a research manager at University of California, Berkeley, before being arrested in 1988 for manufacturing LSD and spending five years in prison. As for Apperson, he had no previous record and contributed to the scheme by setting up and taking down the lab.

Pickard and Apperson were both found guilty, and while Apperson was given thirty years, Pickard was given two life sentences without possibility of parole. Pickard continues to write and research from behind bars at the U.S. Penitentiary at Tucson, Arizona. There are a number of activists working to get him released, as the many of the excesses of the war on drugs have been reversed in recent years. Though Skinner was granted immunity and eventually left Wamego, he went to prison for kidnapping, torturing and drugging several minors and his former girlfriend.

The former missile silo has had quite a history. It is in private hands now, and personal tours can be arranged with the owner by appointment. Just be sure to wave at the neighbors as you drive by.

BASEBALL STAR WITH A DARK SECRET

In the late nineteenth and early twentieth centuries, there stood two kinds of sports stars who shined above all others: boxers and baseball players. Future rival sports such as basketball and football had not been fully developed and sat many years away from drawing large numbers of fans. Major league baseball teams exploded in popularity across the midwestern and northeastern states after the 1870s and many players such as pitcher Cy Young, diminutive hitter Willie Keeler and catcher Buck Ewing became stars. Just like today, though, many players of note crashed and burned their careers with public meltdowns and controversies. One such major league baseball player, by the name of William Clinton Bond "Farmer" Weaver, was one of the most colorful—and scandalous—to do so.

Born near Parkersburg, West Virginia, on or around March 23, 1865, Weaver had only four years of formal education, and his mother died when he was eleven. At the young age of eighteen, Weaver married a local girl named Dora Dove Dye, who was only fourteen or fifteen years old when they wed. Soon after, they followed her family and migrated west in 1889, eventually settling in far southwest Kansas in Kearny County. During his later baseball career, the nickname "Farmer" was applied to him as a reference to his 160-acre farm outside of the town of Lakin, where he stayed in the off season.

In 1885, Weaver rose to prominence with his skill as an outfielder by joining an Olathe team and barnstorming across the state. He played with the Topeka Capitals, the Wellington Browns and the Wichita Braves, and he hopped to teams in Joplin, Missouri, and later to Texas, to make a living. After playing with the Austin, Texas Senators, he was finally making a name for himself and reached the major leagues at the age of twenty-three in 1888, playing for the Louisville Colonels. His batting average of .278 and other skills as a catcher and infielder kept him in the league, and he played 756 games across seven seasons, ending his major league career with the Pittsburgh Pirates in 1894.

Not just excelling as a switch-hitter, Weaver also grew into a prolific baserunner, stealing 162 bases in those seven years. He never became a superstar like Willie Keeler or Ty Cobb but was well known enough to continue his baseball career in a series of other leagues in the ensuing years. He also claimed one phenomenal major league achievement: hitting for the cycle with six hits in one regulation game. This means he hit a single, double, triple and home run, plus two more hits. The next player to match this feat didn't do it until 2009, when Ian Kinsler of the Texas Rangers had the game of his life.

For more than thirty years, Weaver stayed in the game any way that he could, whether as a manager, player or umpire. Over the year, his career took him on a dizzying whirlwind to many teams across different leagues. Over the next decade, he played for the original Milwaukee Brewers of the Class A Western League, the Denver Grizzlies, Salt Lake White Wings, Butte Miners, Boise Fruit Pickers, San Francisco Pirates, Vancouver Veterans and even the Cleveland Spiders. He often pulled ridiculous stunts, such as during

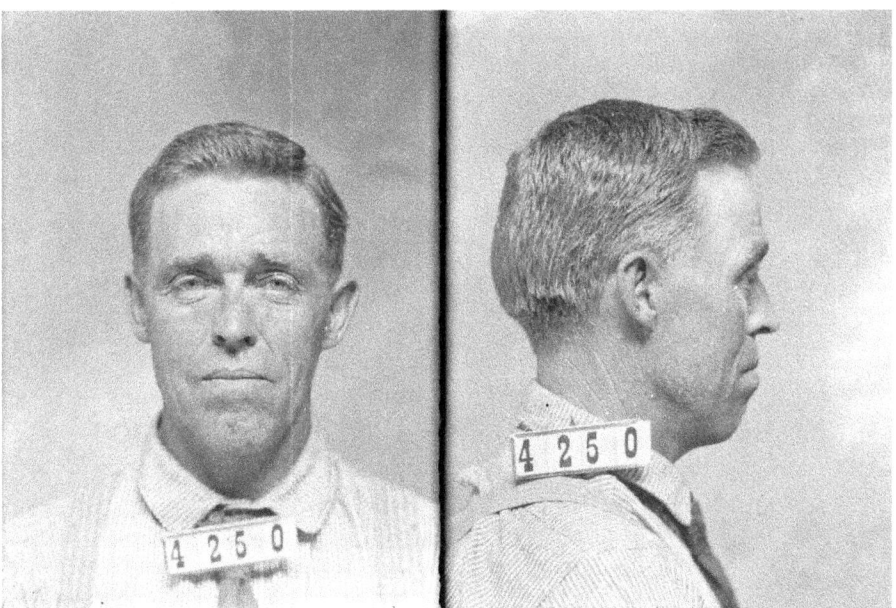

William B. "Farmer" Weaver, March 11, 1912. *Courtesy of Kansas Historical Society.*

a game on July 4, 1893, when he pulled out a pistol and emptied the gun's chamber at a ball descending toward him in the outfield. His bullets missed, but he still fielded the ball, causing a sensation.

Though Weaver had a successful, if unremarkable career as a baseball player, his personal life was often tumultuous. He and Dora adopted an orphan named Cecille Price in September 1901, but their home life was anything but stable. He had a hot temper, which led to many fights, and he filed for divorce in October 1904, alleging infidelity on her part. He withdrew the divorce petition in March 1905, but they remained estranged. She stayed in Boise while he and Cecille lived in Kansas until 1909, when he filed for divorce again. She made a cross petition, claiming to the court that he abused, beat and threatened to kill her. She asked for the divorce on the basis of adultery and extreme cruelty. Weaver, by this time, was something of a Kansas celebrity, and this was at odds with his easy and friendly relations with the fans. In May 1910, a court ruled for Dora, though Cecille remained in her adopted father's custody. Weaver's reputation in Lakin plummeted, and he and Cecille moved to Larned in 1910 so he could manage the Larned Wheat Kings and escape the scrutiny in Lakin.

However, Cecille was pregnant and gave birth to a son in the fall of 1910. Weaver blamed an anonymous Lakin boy, but rumors spread around town at the curious situation of the mysterious pregnancy of the fifteen-year-old girl.

Societal pressure on Weaver's strange situation led him to decide to marry Cecille by the end of the 1911 season. This might have quieted the incessant gossip and brought a conclusion to his legal troubles, but Cecille went to the local authorities with her story. She claimed that he had sexually abused her since she was eleven years old and that he fathered her child, and she told them how afraid of him she was. The Pawnee County sheriff arrested Weaver on November 18, 1911, for violating the state's rape statute. After posting bond, he fled to Mexico a week later. He was captured in El Paso a month later when he came back across the border. The Pawnee County District Court heard his case in March 1912. He pleaded guilty, and the judge ordered him to serve five to twenty-one years.

Arriving at the Kansas State Penitentiary on March 11, 1912, Weaver became inmate no. 4250. Finding baseball to be the most popular thing to do in the prison, he managed one of the prison teams to a twenty-five and three record. He also found a role in the prison's athletic committee, including organizing games against outside non-prisoner teams. One of the games this committee drew up was held on May 30, 1914, between teams from Lansing and Leavenworth Penitentiaries. It stands as the first time a prison had ever hosted inmates from another prison in an athletic contest. The Leavenworth team was made up of all black players and called themselves the "Booker Ts."

To Weaver's great luck, Democrat George Hodges won election as governor of Kansas by only twenty-nine votes in November 1912. Hodges and his parole clerk, Sam Seaton, had both been teammates with Weaver in Olathe back in the mid-1880s. Governor Hodges signed his parole certificate on December 28, 1914, and the prison released Weaver a few days later. Had he not known Hodges he might have been in prison for many more years. Weaver slipped into anonymity after this, leaving the game of baseball forever. He settled into a blue-collar job at Goodyear in Akron, Ohio, and retired in the 1930s. He lived alone in his final years and died a largely forgotten player on January 23, 1943.

Frank Grigware: The Greatest Escape

Designated as the nation's first federal penitentiary, the United States Penitentiary in Leavenworth opened in 1903. State prisons held federal prisoners until Congress passed legislation in 1895 to build a new federal prison system with three first-generation facilities in Leavenworth, Atlanta and McNeil Island. It was built in a rectangular format, which followed a new trend of correctional facilities and stood in stark difference from cell blocks radiating from a central building. At Leavenworth, the prison cells sat back to back in the middle of the structure, with cell openings facing the outer walls. To build this new kind of prison, incarcerated laborers were conscripted from the nearby United States Disciplinary Barracks, a military facility at the Fort Leavenworth army base.

Construction of this massive facility required not only a huge labor force but also a large amount of materials and a locomotive to bring supplies. The walls alone stand 40 feet above the earth, with another 40 feet under the surface. At 3,030 feet long, the walls enclose 22.8 total acres. The massive rectangular building inside these walls was called the "Big House" or the "Big Top" and gave the prison the distinction of being the largest maximum-security federal prison in America for more than one hundred years.

Since this was a massive structure that took many years—and many phases—to construct, its security situation was somewhat fluid with so many prisoners working as laborers and with a steady flow of supplies coming and going. It was in the midst of these changes that a Nebraskan named Frank Grigware pulled off one of the greatest and most successful prison breaks in United States history. The Omaha native was arrested on November 19, 1909, for robbing a mail train and threatening the lives of the mail clerks with a gun. Handed an extremely harsh sentence of life in prison with hard labor at Leavenworth, he vowed to find a way to escape. Being no fool, he studied the comings and goings of construction supplies and the daily patterns of the locomotive that brought them and hatched an escape plan with some other inmates.

On April 21, 1910, Grigware and five others made their long-planned escape in dramatic fashion. After fooling the guards with a piece of wood that they carved into the shape of a gun, the group hijacked the supply locomotive and busted out the prison gates. Twenty-five armed guards and more than two hundred local farmers joined the hunt for the fugitives. Fanning out into the countryside, four of the men were captured within a few hours. A fifth made it for a few days, leaving only Grigware at large. The massive manhunt continued, and the warden of the prison put out a fifty-dollar reward for anyone who could capture and return him.

Agents of the Bureau of Investigation, the national precursor to the FBI, followed many leads that took them all over the nation. Tips rolled in saying people had seen him in numerous states under several different aliases and identities—even as a mechanic, a salesman and a Roman Catholic priest. This manhunt became a national story, and many agents were obsessed with finding him. Was he in New York? Had he fled to Florida? Was he laying low with friends in Nebraska? All of these leads came up empty.

As mentioned before, Grigware was no fool and made the smart move of getting far, far away and moving to northern Alberta, Canada. He changed his name to James Fahey and started a new life for himself. Turning over a new leaf and wanting to avoid more trouble, he stayed busy constructing homes, running a confectioner's store, making friends and becoming active in a local church. He even won election as mayor of the small town of Spirit River in 1916 after moving there the year earlier. The years went by as the Bureau's leads came and went, and in the meantime, our intrepid fugitive got married and began a family. World War I distracted the bureau from such investigations, and the case went cold for many years.

In 1928, Grigware's case was opened again, and the next year, agents learned of a potential sighting of him in Edmonton from ten years earlier. Copies of his fingerprints and photo were sent to the Royal Canadian Mounted Police, but the case sat in limbo for four years before being closed again in 1933. The bureau closed the case again, though he was still noted as "wanted" in official files. Just three months later, after the case was closed, he was caught poaching in Canada and fingerprinted by local Canadian police. The local police mailed his fingerprints to the Mounted Police, where an eagle-eyed clerk matched them to the prints mailed by the United States authorities years before.

Grigware's capture caused a media sensation, and the United States government requested his extradition. He became a popular cause for many Canadians who thought he was likely innocent of his original charges and that he had long ago turned his life around. Thousands of pro-mercy petitions arrived at government offices in Ottawa and Washington, D.C., and the United States dropped the extradition request the next year.

His extradition to the United States being dropped was a massive relief for Grigware, but his case remained open all the way until 1965. The pursuit of him lasted more than half a century and involved several U.S. presidents and even a new bureau, the FBI. A relative of his even requested for him to

Scene of the murder of Viola Ard, 1914. *Courtesy of Kansas Historical Society.*

be allowed to return to the United States to visit family in the late 1950s, but it was denied by the Department of Justice because he was never officially pardoned and remained a fugitive. Grigware lived to the ripe old age of ninety-one and died in 1977. He had lived sixty-seven years as a free man.

The exemplary life that he built showed he was no longer a menace to society, but his case shows how far the art of criminal investigation had come. Investigators learned a lot about the emerging science of fingerprinting and began to establish more formalized transnational law enforcement agreements. Though unsuccessful at bringing him in, the FBI learned a lot from one of its earliest, and longest-running, cases. It also trained local Kansas investigators in the latest tips in the art of fingerprint and forensic firearm analysis. When a young wife, Viola Ard, was mysteriously shot and killed while driving across a bridge near Iola in 1914, these methods were employed to try to crack the case. The prison system learned a thing or two as well—mainly to be careful when constructing prison additions while there are still prisoners around and to be sure to lock up those trains.

3
POLITICS

COUNTY SEAT WARS: A KANSAS TRADITION

When one thinks of political violence in Kansas history, we often think of Bleeding Kansas and the dramatic struggle between pro- and antislavery settlers in the 1850s. Or we might fast forward and think of more modern passions with the assassination of Dr. George Tiller by an antiabortion extremist in Wichita in 2009. What often gets forgotten, however, are the numerous bloody instances of what we might now see as a quaint struggle over county seats.

As Kansas was rapidly expanding in the 1860s and 1870s, new laws were drafted to regularize county incorporation. Once the population of a proposed county rose to six hundred people, the citizens of said area could send a petition to the governor to choose a settlement to act as temporary county seat. The governor would also provide temporary officials to serve until the county was officially formed. Naturally, this led to rivalries between competing settlements vying for the great benefit of being selected.

The benefits of landing a county seat could do wonders for a town. Not only would there be the prestige and economic boom of a courthouse, but there would also be infrastructure that would follow. With a county seat, a town would be a magnet for all farmers, legislators, voters and everyday citizens to do business. With such pull, there would be more business opportunities to serve visitors, which would lead to job openings, and that

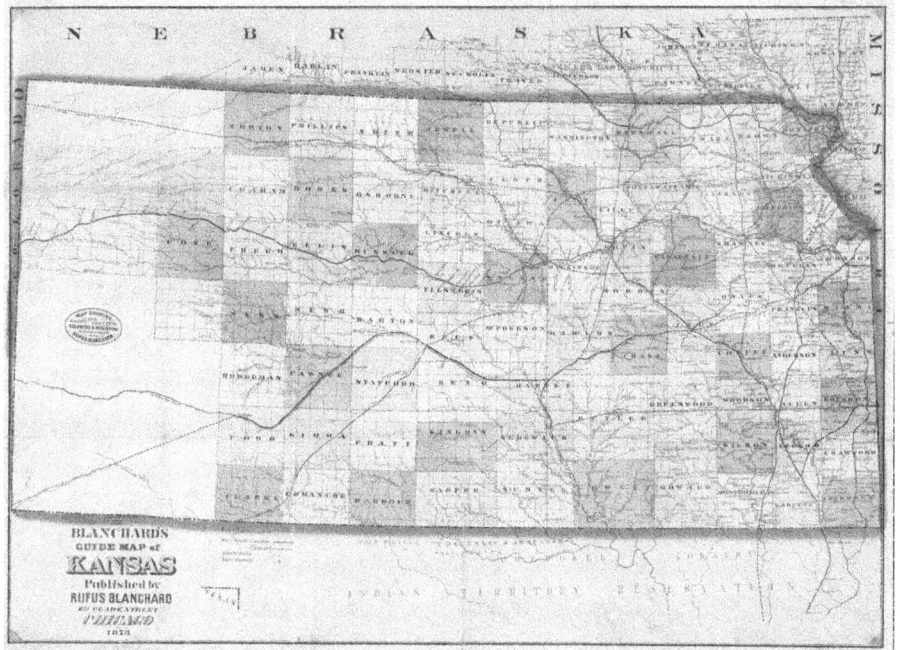

Map of the state of Kansas, 1873. Western counties and towns were still in the process of being organized at this time. *Courtesy of Library of Congress.*

would lead to more schools, investment and even possibly a railroad hub. Winning this prize was so consequential that towns would often die if they were not selected, as people and commerce would drift to the selected town.

Disputes naturally arose over locations of county seats in many places across the state. Echoing the Bleeding Kansas era, elections were often rigged—bribery, backroom deal-making and violence marred many of them. Lawsuits flourished, and fraud was rampant. Passions ran high, especially among men who had made sizeable investments in one town or another and were determined to get their way.

One such instance of passions getting completely out of hand and spilling into violence was the Stevens County War in southwest Kansas. With the rise of rival towns Hugoton and Woodsdale, parties from each town worked to rig the census of their towns, intimidate opposing leaders and even arrest and host mock trials against them. Months of escalating tensions and confrontations led to the bloodiest county seat incident in U.S. history.

In late July 1888, a party of Hugoton county seat supporters led by their marshal, Sam Robinson, planned an outing across the state line into a territory called "No Man's Land," which we now know as the Oklahoma Panhandle. At the time, it was a place without a government, as Oklahoma was not even a state yet, so it was a largely wild and lawless strip of land. Learning of this planned outing, Marshal Ed Short of Woodsdale organized some armed men to intercept and attack them. The Woodsdale men caught up with Robinson, but he managed to escape. With trouble afoot, Robinson hurried back to Hugoton to gather reinforcements.

Temporarily stymied in their attempt to capture Robinson and find the rest of the Hugoton party, Short and the Woodsdale men decided to hunker down for the night of July 25. They camped in a hay meadow near Wild Horse Lake—right over the Kansas border in No Man's Land. In the meantime, Robinson's friends had already organized a posse to go find the Woodsdale camp. Surrounding them at the hay meadow, they opened fire on Robinson's would-be captors and killed four of them and wounded a fifth.

Riding off, the Hugoton posse thought they killed all the Woodsdale group and returned to town saying there had been a shootout. The lone survivor and some other witnesses claimed that the Woodsdale party had been disarmed and summarily executed with no shootout happening. Word quickly spread of this shocking lawlessness, and the state militia was sent out. Several the Hugoton men were arrested.

The state courts couldn't hear the case because the incident happened over the border in No Man's Land. The case had to be tried before the United States Court for the Eastern District in Paris, Texas, and seven men were found guilty of murder and handed death sentences. The case was appealed and eventually went all the way to the Supreme Court, where it was determined that Texas didn't have jurisdiction over the strip either. In the end, no convictions were upheld, and through this technicality, a massacre ended with all perpetrators walking.

Another such situation during this era—just two counties away—also quickly devolved into bloodshed and is now known as the Gray County War. In the Gray County seat election of 1887, there were three similar-sized towns competing to be selected as county seat. Competition was fierce between the towns of Ingalls, Montezuma and Cimarron, and many characters were trying to tip the scales.

Millionaire Asa T. Soule stepped in to put his finger on the scales in this fight. Soule was a New Yorker who made his fortune as the "Hop Bitters King" by patenting and promoting a medicine made of hop bitters. He had money to throw around; he sponsored a baseball team called the Rochester

Hop Bitters in 1879 and later invested in a failed canal to bring Arkansas River water to western Kansas. With this fortune, he founded the town of Ingalls and openly bribed citizens of Montezuma to withdraw their petition and change their vote to Ingalls by passing out checks of $100 to $500. Since $100 was roughly worth $2,500 in 2019 terms, and $500 would now be worth nearly $13,000, you can understand why someone might take that bribe! Not only did he monetarily bribe them, but he also promised to build a railroad through the town, which would be a major commercial benefit in the future.

Soule's scheme ultimately failed, and Cimarron prevailed in the election. Ingalls protested the results, and Cimarron claimed fraud, sending the matter to the Kansas Supreme Court. In the meantime, an Ingalls man, Newt Watson, was elected as the new Gray County clerk. He demanded that the county records at the courthouse in Cimarron be brought to him in Ingalls, which the citizens of Cimarron naturally refused to do. Tensions were mounting, and a group of Ingalls men organized a raiding party to swoop into Cimarron and take the records themselves.

Bill Tilghman stepped up to lead the raiders, but the group comprised some other interesting individuals as well. Jim Masterson, the brother of famed lawman Bat Masterson of Dodge City, joined them along with Fred Singer, Ben Daniels and Neal Brown—all former Dodge City peace officers. Three other men named Brooks, Bolds and Allensworth rounded out the group. The group was further legitimized by the fact that Watson temporarily appointed Tilghman as Gray County sheriff. Tilghman, in turn, deputized the whole group, making their authority concrete in their eyes.

On January 12, 1889, the group arrived by wagon at the courthouse in Cimarron to seize the records. As Watson, Singer, Masterson and Allensworth rushed into the building to grab the papers, the other men waited by the getaway wagon. Taking notice of the situation, a few armed Cimarron men started taking up positions around the courthouse to thwart the raiders. While half the group was still inside, the Cimarron men began opening fire on the men by the wagon. Tilghman was hit in the leg, Bolds was struck twice in the abdomen and once in the leg and Brooks was hit as well. Even the wagon driver, Charlie Reicheldeffer, was hit, but they all jumped in the wagon and quickly retreated out of town, injured but alive. They abandoned their comrades in the courthouse.

Hearing the commotion outside, Masterson and the others inside took positions near the windows on the second floor and prepared for the Cimarron men to rush the building. The raiders' shots discouraged the

Cimarron men's attempts to enter through the front door, and they threw a ladder up in the rear of the building. Masterson noticed this new attempt and kicked the ladder over. Not to be discouraged, the Cimarron men eventually got into the first floor and began firing at the second floor through the ceiling, forcing the raiders to scamper on desks, steel safes and any other thick furniture and cabinets to protect themselves from the bullets below.

As this battle waged for nearly six hours, the rest of the Ingalls men got back to their town and notified Bat Masterson in Dodge City. Masterson sent a telegram to the Cimarron faction threatening to "hire a train and come in with enough men to blow Cimarron off the face of Kansas" if they did not let his brother and the other men leave town. This defused the situation, and the raiders surrendered. They were temporarily taken prisoner before being released.

In all, one man, J.W. English, was killed and three were wounded on the Cimarron side, and four were wounded on the Ingalls side. The raiders were later tried for the murder of English, but all received acquittals. The county seat dispute continued, though bloodlessly, until February 1893, when Cimarron was officially certified as the county seat. The old Gray County courthouse still exists in downtown Cimarron, though it was replaced in 1927. The original is in the National Register of Historic Places, and the public still uses it as a meeting hall.

Not to be outdone by Gray and Stevens Counties, Wichita County had its own violent incident on February 27, 1887. Situated about two miles apart, the towns of Leoti and Coronado both grew quickly and sprouted thriving businesses, such as newspapers, hotels and mercantile stores. When Kansas governor John Alexander Martin was petitioned in 1886 to appoint a census taker, the competition commenced. With an official count of legal voters on the horizon, the fates of both towns were at stake.

Each town's newspapers hurled invective at the others as tensions flared, and boosters of each community ratcheted up the tension, with run-ins and fistfights becoming common occurrences. Armed cowboys even shot up downtown Leoti one day, filling the post office and other businesses with bullet holes and humiliating businessmen by forcing them to do an Irish jig on Main Street while they shot at their feet.

The much-anticipated preliminary election was set for February 8, 1887 and was rife with fraud and illegality. Many votes were bought for upward of fifty dollars a man, and men from outside the county filled the voter rolls. Thuggish armed cowboys patrolled the polling places, intimidating many potential voters. Add that to scores of fictitious names on the voting

The Dodge City Peace Commission, 1883. Lawmen in Dodge City were often called out to other communities to keep the peace over the years. Members are identified as *(back row, left to right)* William H. Harris, Luke Short, William Bat Masterson, W.F. Petillon; *(front row, left to right)* Charles E. Bassett, Wyatt Earp, Frank McLain, Neil Brown. *Courtesy of Kansas Historical Society.*

rolls, and you had a recipe for violence. Leoti was declared the temporary county seat before the actual county seat election on March 10, 1887. A town named Farmer City, near both Leoti and Coronado, was offered as a compromise county seat, but the idea was rejected by both sides.

The tension hadn't abated, and on February 27, a wagon with seven armed, liquored-up Leoti men rode to Main Street in Coronado for some "fun." After shooting up the town and generally having a great time at their rivals' expense, the Leoti men were surprised when the Coronado men aimed rifles out of the upper floor windows of their downtown businesses and rained bullets upon them. As they ran to their wagon to beat a hasty retreat, many bullets began to hit their marks. Leoti men George Watkins, William Raines and purported ex-Quantrill raider Charles Coulter fell from the wagon, dead. Another, Frank Jenness, was hit six times and died later. Three others were hit in various parts of their bodies, but all lived. One man, Emmet Denning, had to have a leg amputated.

The Wichita County sheriff was completely overwhelmed by this escalation of violence and sent desperate telegrams to Topeka. The governor called out the Kansas Militia. Companies from Sterling and Larned headed out. Lawmen from Dodge City, including notables Wyatt Earp, Pat Sughrue, Bill Tilghman and Bat Masterson, were posted at Coronado to keep any of the killers from slipping town before the militia arrived. The militia also dug rifle pits around the Leoti town hall. This became the biggest military action in this part of the state since the Cheyenne Indian Raid of 1879.

Colonel Rickseker, the leader of the contingent sent to Coronado, sternly warned the armed men of the town that he was in a foul mood and they would be wise to lay down their arms and surrender to the authorities. Doing so, he arrested twenty-one Coronadoans, charged them with first-degree murder and shipped them to jails in Hays, Garden City and Dodge City. When they were tried in Great Bend a year later, all twenty-one men were acquitted due to insufficient evidence.

Cheyenne Indians who broke out of their reservation when they were dissatisfied with the conditions and raided north into western Kansas, 1879. *Courtesy of New York Public Library.*

Despite all the lawlessness, the March 10 election was still held. The presence of the lawmen and the state militia kept order and discouraged the rampant voter fraud that had happened previously. Leoti triumphed in this election and became the permanent county seat. This bitterness and unnecessary violence soon faded, and hard feelings were soon smoothed over. The Town of Leoti offered free lots to citizens of Coronado, and many of the citizens, and even the buildings, of Coronado moved to Leoti. Coronado and Farmer City are all but gone and have been converted to farmland now. Leoti has remained the dominant community of Wichita County ever since.

Probably the most unexpected result of a county seat struggle is the curious case of Garfield County. In 1887, the towns of Eminence and Ravanna were locked in a similar bitter dispute, and Dodge City sent Bat Masterson and twenty deputized men to keep the peace during their election. The election was rife with fraud (of course!) with thousands of votes cast, though each town had a population of fewer than four hundred people. Ravanna won by thirty-five votes, but Eminence sued. The Kansas Supreme Court declared Eminence the winner, and the county seat moved there.

The joke was on both of them, though. In 1892, the court took a closer look at Garfield County after citizens requested a survey. The Kansas State Constitution requires counties to be at least 432 square miles, and when the court realized Garfield was too small and had been illegally organized, it was annexed by Finney County in 1893. Finney County owes its large and unique shape to this ruling. Eminence and Ravanna are ghost towns now, and the limestone ruins of former schools and a courthouse give mute testimony to their past existence.

If you're ever driving through the Kansas countryside and come across places like Heartland, Surprise, Kendall or Appomattox, you will pass other losers in long-forgotten county seat wars. Many of these places were the sites of intense passions, bitter rivalries and flying bullets. The next time you see a county courthouse, just remember a time when people fought and died for them.

The Quack Doctor Who Nearly Became Governor

On the night of November 4, 1930, a doctor by the name of John R. Brinkley stood on the cusp of his greatest coup in a life full of schemes, cons and shoot-for-the-moon gambits. Stripped of his license to practice medicine in the state of Kansas, he had thrown his massive wealth into a barnstorming tour of the state to support his campaign to be the state's twenty-fifth governor. Garnering hundreds of thousands of write-in votes, he had a great shot of beating both the Democrat, Harry H. Woolridge, and Republican, Frank Haucke, for the top office. Great forces stood against him, as well as many people in high places working to make sure this "quack" never held office. What made him a quack doctor in the eyes of many, you might ask. Well, Dr. Brinkley had risen to fame and fortune peddling a peculiar and highly dubious treatment for male impotence: the transplantation of goat testicles into humans.

Dr. John R. Brinkley between 1920–40. *Courtesy of Kansas Historical Society.*

Born John Romulus Brinkley on July 8, 1885, in North Carolina to a former Confederate army medic named John Richard Brinkley, the young John lived a hardscrabble life in his early years. Having little money, John Sr. practiced medicine in the mountains of western North Carolina and married four different times. Scandalously, during his marriage to a forty-two-year-old woman named Sarah T. Mingus, her twenty-four-year-old niece, Sarah Candice Burnett, came to live with them and subsequently got pregnant with young John. She died of tuberculosis and pneumonia when he was just five years old, and John's father died when he was ten.

Going to school in a one-room log cabin, Brinkley completed his studies at sixteen and had numerous jobs, including as a mail carrier and a telegraph operator. Working as a telegrapher in New York and New Jersey for a few different railroad companies, he did whatever honest work he could find to get by. He still dreamed of one day becoming a doctor and had tagged along on many house calls that his father had made. In 1906, his life changed when he went home for Sarah T. Mingus's funeral. He reconnected with a schoolmate named Sally Wike, and they married on January 27, 1907. With her encouragement and his dreams of traveling and being a doctor, he began his forays into the medical world.

Traveling around small towns in North Carolina and Tennessee, the newlywed Brinkleys posed as Quaker doctors and promoted dubious patent medicines. He also did public shows promoting "virility tonics" with another man named Dr. Burke. Carnival barkers and outrageous traveling medical shows dominated the town squares and meeting places of this era. Quack doctors and tonics such as these became common sights in cities across the nation, and the rise in the effectiveness and popularity of real medicines made it difficult for the public to tell the difference between the frauds and the real deal.

Moving to Chicago in 1907, the young couple had a daughter named Wanda as John began studies at an unaccredited school called Bennett Medical College. Brinkley still worked as a telegrapher at night while going to his classes during the day, but many of the classes didn't conform to the standard medical education of the time. The school focused heavily on "eclectic" medicine, a practice of medicine focused on botanical and herb-based remedies. One radical course focused an inordinate amount of time on new theories of gland extraction and its effects on the body. He was spellbound by the possibilities of this new medical frontier and determined that it would play a part in his future.

Brinkley's home life brimmed with constant chaos. Sally filed for divorce on one occasion, he kidnapped his daughter and fled to Canada on another and another daughter, Erna, was born in the middle of all of this. They reunited, and he left Chicago with unpaid tuition looming over his head. Moving from North Carolina to Florida and later to Missouri, Brinkley established himself as a sort of "undergraduate physician" with little success. By 1912, he tried to continue his education in St. Louis, but Bennett Medical College refused to forward his records to other medical schools due to the tuition he still owed. After these unsuccessful attempts to be a legitimate doctor, Brinkley enrolled at a dubious institution called the Kansas City Eclectic Medical University, a place widely reputed as a diploma mill. After the birth of another daughter and moves to New York and Chicago, Sally eventually tired of it all and took the girls back home to North Carolina.

Brinkley set up shop in Greenville, South Carolina, with another man named J.E. Crawford. They promoted themselves as "electro-medical doctors" who could help men regain their "vigor, virility and manhood" by drinking what was little more than colored water that they sold for twenty-five dollars a bottle. The business failed, and they skipped town, owing money to many merchants. Fleeing to Memphis, Brinkley married twenty-one-year-old Minerva Jones after a four-day romance. Not long after, he was arrested in Knoxville and extradited back to Greenville, where he blamed it all on Crawford. Settling out of court, Brinkley not only had the humiliation of having his new father-in-law help pay bail, but Sally also confronted the new couple, letting Minnie know that John was practicing bigamy.

Met again and again with financial, professional and marital chaos, Brinkley finally turned a profit in Arkansas, where he took over the office of a doctor who was leaving the state. He paid off his tuition to Bennett Medical University, and in 1914, he moved to Kansas City to finish his schooling at the Eclectic Medical University. It was here that he began studying the prostate glands of older men because he was fascinated by the gland's propensity for enlargement and irritation. Graduating on May 7, 1915, he could now legally practice medicine in eight states. This was the great breakthrough he had been waiting for. Working as a doctor at the local Swift and Company plant, where he studied animal physiology and biology, he took special notice of the strength and health of the common goat. This insight, plus his study of glands, would greatly shape his career.

After serving a short stint in the U.S. Army in 1917 during World War I, Brinkley moved with his new wife and their young son to the town of Milford, Kansas. The town had placed ads in newspapers across Kansas and Missouri to recruit a new doctor, and its leaders were thrilled with their choice when he arrived. In 1918, he opened a sixteen-room clinic in Milford, where he charged reasonable prices, got along with the townsfolk and paid decent wages. With the 1918 influenza pandemic sweeping across the world, Brinkley gained praise from many locals for saving their lives and by making house calls to those afflicted by the virus. In Milford, he achieved a level of success and respect that he had never held in his entire life. He had finally found a safe harbor to drop anchor, and he was off to a great start.

It was at this time that Dr. Brinkley first did what we now know him for: the transplantation of goat testicles into men. According to Brinkley, a patient begged him to help him overcome his "sexual weakness," and Brinkley jested that all he needed was a "pair of those buck [goat] glands in you." He claimed that the desperate patient implored him to try the operation and paid $150. Accounts of this first experiment differ, as the son of that patient later told the *Kansas City Star* that it was actually the other way around and that Brinkley offered to pay the man for partaking in this experiment.

The operations that Brinkley performed were like nothing most people had ever seen before, and he charged $750 (nearly $10,000 in today's money) per procedure. When the goats' testicular glands were placed in the patients, their bodies simply treated the organs as foreign matter. The glands never interacted with the body and were absorbed.

Word of these operations spread after the wife of one of his patients gave birth to a healthy baby boy. The national newspapers that ran the story led to new patients from all over the nation, and he promoted goat glands as a cure for dozens of ailments. He claimed they could even cure such minor problems as excessive flatulence. He hired an advertising man to help him promote the clinic through direct mailers and shipped out thousands of fliers directly to potential customers.

The American Medical Association took notice of his clinic and his fantastical claims and began an investigation. An undercover agent at his clinic saw general uncleanliness, intoxication and even a woman who had been given goat ovaries to cure a tumor. A doctor by the name of Morris Fishbein took specific notice, as he was an expert in uncovering medical fraudsters. Nevertheless, Brinkley's fame and fortune grew, and he even publicly demonstrated his work on thirty-four patients at a Chicago hospital. This event, as well as a successful operation on a *Los Angeles Times* editor, brought scores of new patients—even Hollywood film stars. He dreamed of moving his clinic to California, but the state medical board found his résumé to be riddled with exaggerations and inconsistencies.

With the money rolling in, Brinkley realized that radio could be a powerful and effective way to advertise himself, and in 1923 he founded his own station—Kansas First, Kansas Best (KFKB). This radio station upped his public profile and aided him when he was indicted by a grand jury in San Francisco for receiving a fake medical degree. Agents from California attempted to arrest him, but the governor of Kansas refused to extradite him because he was such a financial boon for the state. He often spoke on the air about how outside forces were trying to bring him down and triumphantly boasted his victory over California. He also used this platform to denounce Fishbein, who had been writing articles calling him a quack in the *Journal of the American Medical Association* (*JAMA*).

Business started booming, and his new hometown of Milford supported him. Pulling in patients from around the world by the mid-1920s, his success allowed him to give back to the community very generously. He paid for new sidewalks, a bandstand, a new sewage system and a post office. He even sponsored a baseball team called the Brinkley Goats. He was earning millions of dollars a year, so he had plenty of cash to throw around by this time.

At the same time, though, Fishbein wrote more in the *JAMA* about patients who got infections and even died from his procedures. Fishbein and others even lobbied foreign governments to rescind fake and honorary degrees given to Brinkley. Benito Mussolini revoked one in Italy, but Brinkley still claimed it on his résumé until the end of his life. The *Kansas City Star* and other publications soon picked up on stories such as these and printed several increasingly damning articles about him. The Kansas Medical Board investigated the fact that Brinkley signed forty-two death certificates at his clinic over the years and discovered that many weren't even sick upon arrival. Concluding that they were the victims of botched surgeries, the board revoked his license. Brinkley's fall had begun.

In the middle of 1930, Brinkley found his empire collapsing all around him and took the only route that could save it: politics. He launched a longshot bid for the governorship of Kansas in the hopes that he could appoint allies to the state medical board and regain his medical license. Having deep pockets and scores of admirers across the state, a Brinkley victory could happen. He took his own plane, *The Romancer*, to dramatically deliver him to his rallies on a statewide tour, which was a huge spectacle for 1930. Promising lower taxes, old-age pensions, free textbooks for schoolchildren and even a state lake in every county, Brinkley struck a nerve with hundreds of thousands of voters across the state.

Great forces stood against him though, as he had many opponents in the state government. Since he didn't announce until September—after ballots had been printed—Brinkley had to make sure his followers wrote him in on their ballots. In a surprise move just three days before the election, the state attorney general announced a new rule that write-in candidates had to have their name written a very specific way—with the first two initials of the name followed by the last name. Only ballots marked "J.R. Brinkley" would be accepted. Ballots with "Dr. Brinkley" or "John Brinkley" or any other version of his name would be discarded. This sneaky trick would have devastating consequences for his candidacy.

Receiving 183,278 votes wasn't enough to make Brinkley governor, and he came in third to winner Democrat Harry Woodring (217,171 votes) and Republican Frank Haucke (216,920 votes). The *Des Moines Register* estimated that 30,000 to 50,000 votes for Brinkley were thrown out due to the rule change. Woodring later admitted that he never would have won if all of Brinkley's votes been counted. Brinkley ran again in 1932, pulling in 244,607 votes, but again came in third to winner Alf Landon, who would go on to lose to Franklin Roosevelt in the 1936 presidential election.

Brinkley had a great run in Kansas, but losing his elections, his medical license and even his station's broadcasting license, which the Federal Radio

Commission refused to renew, he decided to move to Texas. He left two of his apprentices in charge of the practice and headed south to Del Rio, Texas, where he got involved in a border blaster radio station in Mexico, built a mansion, did the occasional goat transplant and still advertised quack concoctions, such as "crazy water crystals."

Morris Fishbein, his old *JAMA* antagonist, published an incredibly damning work called "Modern Medical Charlatans," which included a large report on Brinkley. Brinkley sued for libel, lost big and had to defend himself from a barrage of counter lawsuits concerning medical malpractice. This cost him millions of dollars. The IRS investigated him for tax fraud, and he declared bankruptcy in 1941. The United States Postal Service also opened investigations into mail fraud. His health began to collapse, and he had three heart attacks and had to have a leg amputated due to circulation issues. He died broke in San Antonio on May 26, 1942.

Brinkley's career goes to show the old Jonathan Swift—not Mark Twain—adage "a lie can travel halfway around the world while the truth is still putting on its shoes" applies to many situations. Brinkley had amassed wealth, fame, power and prestige before the rest of the medical world could even catch up. He had detractors from the very start, but it took about twenty years to bring down Brinkley. His popularity and the power of the radio left him largely unchecked, and many people loved him for it. Were it not for a sneaky ballot rule change, Brinkley would likely be remembered as one of the most colorful and controversial governors in Kansas history.

Jason Clarke Swayze: The Fightin-est Newspaperman in Kansas

Many shootouts in Kansas history have occurred as the result of bank robberies, political differences, drunken brawls, disputed county seats and, of course, a man making unwanted advances toward another man's wife. What's exceedingly rare, though, is when two newspapermen draw guns on each other, which happened between Jason Clarke Swayze and John Wilson in Topeka on March 27, 1877.

Hailing from a New Jersey farm, Swayze took up the printing trade as an apprentice at age sixteen and moved around Pennsylvania, New York City and, later, Georgia. Having worked for famed *New York Tribune* publisher Horace Greeley, Swayze had learned from the best and became respected in

Jason Clarke Swayze between 1870–77. *Courtesy of Kansas Historical Society.*

his field. Being a man of strong convictions, and even after his move to Georgia, he still personally stood loyal to the Union during the Civil War. He was taking no small risk when he brought his wife, Kate, and their three children to Georgia,

At the height of the war in August 1863, he printed a four-page folio mocking the Southern view of Abraham Lincoln, which caused a sensation in Griffin, Georgia. A group of Rebel sympathizers and recruiters took possession of his office and rode him on a rail (in which a victim is made to straddle a fence rail supported by the shoulders of two or more people) to the edge of town. Many of the town's citizens jeered at him as they led him off and eventually placed him on a barrel. His tormenters threatened to tar and feather him unless he renounced his affection for the Union and gave a "hurrah for Jeff Davis." He defiantly replied that they could tar, feather or even hang him, but he would never betray his love for the United States. Some of the town's more influential citizens calmed down the crowd and spared him. He was transferred to military custody and imprisoned by the Confederates for a few months before later escaping to Sherman's lines.

It is hard to tell where the truth is in some of Swayze's stories, as he told many acquaintances that he was a Union spy after escaping the South. What is known, however, is the extent of his courage in returning to Griffin after the war. Still a proud and defiant Republican, he had many enemies in the area. In 1867, six of the "best citizens" in town walked into his office with a rope and told him they would hang him from the first limb they could find. He coolly pulled two Colt seven-shooters from a drawer and ran them off.

In 1873, he decided to leave Georgia because the market for a staunchly Republican newspaper proved nonexistent. Relocating to Topeka, he brought his defiant attitude and absolute devotion to printing his firm opinions, no matter who it offended. He established the *Topeka Blade*, another firebrand newspaper, and he vowed to "cut off rotten limbs, shield innocence and virtue and aid the stalwart arm of the farmer and mechanic." Swayze believed that his mission was to be a beacon of truth in a world full of liars and scoundrels.

It didn't take long before Swayze began to castigate fellow journalists from rival newspapers in Topeka. He took aim at longtime *Topeka Times* editor and former Kansas state senator Veal Porter Wilson. This led Wilson's twenty-four-year-old son, John, to uphold his father's honor and punch Swayze to the ground in an altercation on a Topeka street on March 10, 1877. John Wilson, who later worked for the *Topeka Commonwealth* across the street from the *Topeka Blade*, would often see Swayze on the street. The two men were always in close proximity in the area of Sixth and South Kansas Avenues in downtown Topeka.

The final straw was when Swayze insulted John Wilson by deeming him "a gambler and a pimp" in an article and implicated him and a number of prominent men in a lottery scandal. Wilson had enough and walked with a constable toward the *Topeka Blade* office on the evening of March 27, 1877, to have a talk about it. Meeting at Post Office Alley, the men became belligerent and began a shootout. Shooting at each other nearly instantaneously, Wilson was grazed in the cheek by a bullet and Swayze was hit in the chest. The forty-four-year-old Swayze slumped to the ground, dead. Swayze had attempted a second shot at Wilson, but his pistol misfired. He left behind a second wife and five children.

Wilson was acquitted of murder and manslaughter at the ensuing trial, as both men were armed and the authorities saw it as an honor duel. Many newspapers across the state condemned the act, but the March 30, 1877 edition of the *Emporia News* stated,

> *The handkerchief trade has increased largely in Kansas City and Leavenworth, since the verdict acquitting Wilson. The demand comes from the briny condition of the eyes of those lovely and innocent individuals who edit the twin paper,* the Kansas City *and* Leavenworth Times. *They weep and refuse to be comforted over the degeneracy of society in Topeka. The freedom of the press and security to life is all gone, because a man, in self-defense, rid society of a public pest. Bah!*

Swayze, to this day, is the only journalist killed by another journalist in Kansas history. Two years later, his *Topeka Blade* became the *Topeka State Journal*, which lasted for more than one hundred years. It merged in 1981 with the *Topeka Daily Capital* and today still exists as the *Topeka Capital-Journal*. Swayze left his mark on Topeka, as a descendant of his newspaper still survives.

Triple Play of 1956

Some great synonyms for the word "wicked" are "immoral," "wrong" and "unscrupulous." Not every seedy tale from Kansas history could necessarily be defined as evil, but many are corrupt and objectionable. One such act openly played out in public and involved a plan to rig the Kansas Supreme Court.

Joining the Union in 1861, Kansas followed the norm of many other states in which elected judges made up the judiciary. Since such closeness existed between the parties and the judges, many reform movements cropped up over the ensuing decades to try to make the courts as nonpartisan as possible. The three levels of general jurisdiction courts—supreme court, court of appeals and district court—were all susceptible to partisan takeover and biased rulings depending on which party held power.

By the 1950s, the governor still appointed judges to the Kansas Supreme Court, much like the U.S. Supreme Court justices are appointed by the U.S. president. In 1956, the incumbent governor Fred Hall lost the Republican primary to a challenger named Warren Shaw, who subsequently lost the general election to Democrat George Docking. On December 31, as Hall rode out his lame duck governorship until January, the chief justice of the Supreme Court, William A. Smith, decided to retire due to ill health.

Not wanting the next governor—a Democrat—to appoint the next justice, Hall conspired with his lieutenant governor, John B. McCuish, and sitting Kansas Supreme Court chief justice, William Smith, to game the system. Being a big supporter of Hall, Smith didn't want Docking to appoint a Democrat if he retired. The die had been cast. With just two weeks left in his governorship, Hall resigned as governor on January 3, 1957, elevating McCuish as the state's thirty-fourth governor. McCuish's only official act as governor was to turn around and appoint the recently resigned former governor, Hall, to the recently vacated chief justice seat. The public and the press were outraged, and this action became known as the "Triple Play of 1956." Though this technically wasn't illegal, it was considered highly unethical and corrupt. It reeked of back-room deal making and reminded many people of the era of Boss Tweed and Tammany Hall.

Being so incensed by this move, the Kansas legislature passed a resolution in 1957 to amend the state constitution and reform the appointment of judges. The amendment was put to a vote in the 1958 general election, and it passed. The Kansas Bar Association lobbied hard and won a merit-based system for selecting supreme court justices. With merit selection,

John Berridge McCuish, the eleven-day governor, 1957. *Courtesy of Kansas Historical Society.*

when a vacancy opened on the state supreme court, the nonpartisan Kansas Supreme Court nominating commission would review applications for the seat and submit three of the most qualified candidates to the governor. Each candidate would be a licensed attorney with activity as a judge, lawyer or law teacher at an accredited law school for at least ten years. Much like a job interview, the applicants would not only be interviewed but would also have their references checked and qualifications examined.

This system was designed to allow the best legal minds to rise to the top. The nominating commission would be made of nine members, including a lawyer and non-lawyer from each of the state's four congressional districts, plus a lawyer to chair the group. The commission would take all applications and vote by secret ballot to narrow its list to between six and eight names. It would then propose three of those candidates to the governor. This merit plan later extended to district and appeals courts, with districts having the option to have either merit or partisan selection processes. Most judicial districts chose merit selection.

All this work to make a less partisan system stood for fifty-five years until 2013, when Governor Sam Brownback and the Kansas legislature voted to replace the court of appeals merit selection process with the old system of gubernatorial appointment. Current governor Laura Kelly has opted to go back to the merit-based system in the appellate courts, so it appears that this system might make a comeback, at least for the moment. The merit selection process is still supported by a majority of Kansans in polls, all thanks to a sneaky deal more than fifty years ago.

And how did that deal work out for former governor Hall, you might ask? He sat on the state supreme court until the next year, 1958, when he resigned and aimed to win back the governorship. He lost in the primary and decided to retire from politics forever and go into the business world. His triple play was a brilliant stroke of political maneuvering, but it harmed his credibility with the public and damaged the esteem Kansans had for the supreme court. It did, however, lead to reforms that ultimately strengthened the courts in the eyes of many. So, in the case of the Triple Play, three wrongs made a right.

4
VIGILANTE JUSTICE

The Lynching of Nat Oliphant

One of the ugliest chapters in American history is the era of lynching between the end of the Civil War and the 1960s. Lynchings are often thought of as hangings, but they took many forms. Defined as an extrajudicial act of murder by a group of people, victims were not always just hanged but also burned alive, shot, tortured or forced to jump from great heights. The vast majority of lynchings were perpetrated against African American men to preserve white supremacy, but women and whites were also lynched, depending on the situation. These killings happened in every state, even California, Maine and Delaware. The Tuskegee Institute counted 4,743 lynchings between 1882 and 1968, with 54 of those occurring in Kansas. Of those, 35 were white men who had been accused of crimes such as horse theft, rape and, in the case of Nat Oliphant, murder.

Just after three o'clock on the morning of June 4, 1889, a well-respected and successful Topekan tailor named Alonzo T. Rodgers was roused from his sleep by Nat Oliphant, who was a drifter in town and committed burglaries where he could. The men couldn't be any more different. Oliphant was described by witnesses and the local newspaper as an unkempt and "tough-looking individual" with dirty, wrinkled clothes and a face full of dirty stubble. Rodgers was a forty-three-year-old businessman with a wife, Malvina, and two daughters, Rebecca (six) and Mary (two months).

Oliphant entered the house through an unsecure door and went upstairs with a handgun. Rebecca had woken her father with her coughing, as she was sick, and he left his room to go across the hall and check on her. Just then, Oliphant and Rodgers collided in the dark. Oliphant shot Rodgers in the stomach after Rodgers grabbed him. Malvina heard the commotion and walked out. She grappled with the intruder and was shot in the stomach as well. Their maid, Mary Klinkerman, was also in the home and rushed to aid in the struggle. Mr. Rodgers was shot again—this time in the left arm—and Malvina bit Oliphant's hand while Klinkerman went for his throat. Rodgers seized the gun from Oliphant and beat him over the head with it before relenting and telling Oliphant to leave. Amazingly, he told Oliphant that he would "be more merciful to you than you were to me" before the burglar left.

Oliphant, knowing this story would spread, went straight to the Kansas River and dropped his blood-stained clothes into the water and washed off the Rodgerses' blood. He proceeded to walk east toward Tecumseh, intending to catch a train there at daylight. Two Topeka police officers apprehended him in Tecumseh when they noticed him wearing only an undershirt—which was very not common in public in those days—and hiding in some brush. Alonzo died later that morning, but Malvina recovered from her wounds.

When he was taken to the station, Oliphant confessed not only to the murder of Rodgers but also to several other local burglaries. Mr. Rodgers had a reputation as a beloved and respected member of the Topeka business community, and after the *Daily Capital* ran a report of this "cold blooded" murder, a crowd began gathering around the jail at Southwest Fifth and Van Buren that evening. This crowd was described by the local paper as lacking any "hoodlum element," and "lawyers, merchants, bankers and other businessmen gathered in knots and discussed the situation and the unanimous opinion was that the wretch ought to hang. The idea that he might be innocent was scouted from the moment the servant girl identified Oliphant as the murderer." This cannot be viewed as unruly anarchy, but as a premeditated act by the leading men of the city. Such was the commonality of lynching in the nineteenth-century United States.

By nine o'clock at night, the crowd was estimated to be nearly fifteen thousand people strong. This was about half of the population of the city. Chants that the scoundrel should hang erupted from the crowd. The state had not executed anyone in more than fifteen years, so members of the crowd wanted to take the matter into their own hands.

Several Topeka officers and deputies attempted to stop the crowd from entering the jail, but the crowd pushed the guards aside with a wooden

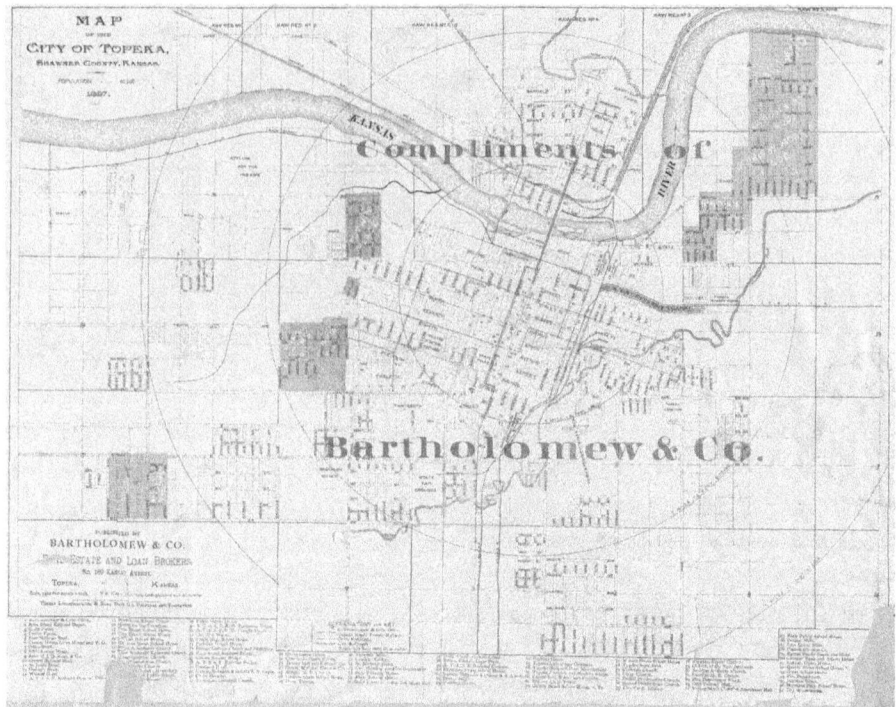

Map of Topeka, Kansas, in 1887. With a population of forty thousand, it was a relatively small town in many ways. The fact that fifteen thousand people—nearly half the town—attended the lynching of Nat Oliphant is an astounding testament to the normalization of this practice at the time. *Courtesy of New York Public Library.*

plank. The chief of police, J.W. Gardiner, was knocked unconscious, and the sheriff, A.M. Fuller, was also injured in the melee. The crowd would not be denied, and they quickly found Oliphant and figured out how to open his cell door. Dragging him from the building in an angry and loud frenzy, the vigilantes strung a rope around his neck, and one person gave him a tremendous punch after he attempted to escape. From then on, he struggled no more.

Oliphant knew that he was doomed and beseeched the crowd for a minister. After one came forward, he tried to pull the rope from Oliphant's neck and defuse the mob's blood lust. The mob wasn't having it and quickly replaced the rope. By eleven o'clock, they had taken him half a block east of Sixth and Topeka Avenues and had thrown the other end of his rope over a telegraph pole crossbar. He was quickly pulled upward and showed no fear or repentance as his body rocked back and forth. One member of the crowd shot the body.

Lynching of Nat Oliphant, June 4, 1889. *Courtesy of Kansas Historical Society.*

Articles about the lynching peppered the state with headlines such as "Crazed with Anger" and "Avenged," noting the crowd's reaction to the murder. Rather than waiting for a trial and due process, the citizens of Topeka ensured that Nat Oliphant was dead not twelve hours after Mr. Rodgers. Oliphant's body was cut down and taken to the nearest morgue, where it was displayed for the public. This is the first, and only, public lynching on record in Topeka and Shawnee County as a whole.

We usually equate lynchings with a racial element and the Jim Crow South, but this episode reveals that they were also sometimes seen as acts of public good by leading citizens. They acted as a sort of morality play that the entire population could witness and be a part of. Public executions had been a common sight from colonial times to the late 1800s, so the perpetrators of this violence would not have seen this as anything out of the ordinary. To them, it represented righting a wrong that they didn't trust the state to properly address. We look at these acts from today as barbarism and lawlessness of the highest order, but it's important to keep in mind that many at the time saw it as completely normal.

Atchison Mob Lynches Nearly Entire Gang

Kansas was a wild place during the year 1863. The energies of nearly the entire citizenry of the two-year-old state focused on supporting the Union effort in the Civil War. Having recently lived through the Bleeding Kansas era, and still grappling with Bushwhacker and Confederate threats, there were natural disruptions as many of the men shipped off to war. With the chaos of the war raging, and unsettled nerves among the citizenry, vigilante justice became an entirely acceptable solution to many citizens. In Atchison, one unlucky gang learned this lesson the hard way.

On May 16, the Kelseys, a farm family, were assaulted at their country home by a group of ten or eleven men. Similar to the Clutter murders nearly one hundred years later, this gang thought that the father, Arthur Kelsey, might have $2,000 (nearly $40,000 in today's money) for recently herding some cattle for the U.S. government for the war effort. Claiming that they didn't have anywhere near that kind of money, the Kelseys pleaded with the men to leave them in peace. The gang would have none of it and even tortured their twelve-year-old son in a futile attempt to get him to tell where the money was hidden.

Realizing this assault was fruitless, the thieves took several possessions from the family, including flour, bacon, clothing and, most importantly, their four horses. The only cash they went away with was forty dollars. After that, they fled the scene but weren't wise enough to leave town. Word spread fast though, and locals pieced together which young men happened to be gone that night at the time of the robbery. The citizens of the town summarily apprehended eleven of the robbers and took them to the jail.

Two of the inmates were well-known local brothers, William and Porter Sterling, aged twenty-two and twenty-five, respectively. They were quickly identified by the Kelsey family as two of the perpetrators. The combination of the frontier setting and the backdrop of the Civil War led the town to throw together a mock jury to try the case. Five jurors were selected from the town and seven from the countryside. The Sterlings admitted to their guilt, and the jury decided that they would be hanged not two days after the robbery. On Monday, May 18, a large mob took them by wagon from the jail to a nearby sturdy tree limb. Tying up their arms, the mob told the brothers to "prepare for death." William, the younger brother, hanged first while Porter watched. Porter's wife intervened and pleaded with the lynching party to spare his life because he had, up until then, lived a good and industrious life. Miraculously, the wife's pleas turned the crowd toward mercy and Porter was allowed to live.

Though Porter lucked out, the rest of the gang was not in the clear yet. The next day, May 19, another man, Henry "Pony" McCarthy, the youngest member of the gang at eighteen years old, was captured and imprisoned at the Atchison County Jail. Authorities apprehended a middle-aged associate of theirs named Daniel Mooney as well. Another mob lynched Pony that very day, but they delayed Mooney's lynching for reasons lost to history. Mooney sat in jail and avoided the mob for a few more days, but by May 23, impatient citizens moved to string up the remaining robbers. Mooney and thirty-five-year-old Alexander Brewer received a mock trial between ten o'clock in the morning and five in the evening, and each man claimed the other was the more guilty party. The jury took both at their word and condemned both to die.

The size of this lynch mob was estimated by the local newspaper to be between three and five thousand people. This bloodthirsty crowd took Mooney and Brewer to the very tree where William Sterling was hanged. Their deaths brought the mob's body count to four. Some sources say that another man, Edward Gilbert, was hanged, though others say that he escaped from the Atchison County Jail and never returned to town. One other source even says that Porter Sterling was not spared and was hanged as well.

This story highlights the dubious reliability of witnesses to history. Lynchings as a practice were an unofficial act, with no paperwork or officialdom to record them, so gathering the facts can be difficult. What's amazing is that this was seen as a completely normal way to bring order and justice to a lawless situation. To the citizens at the time, it was a necessary evil that just "needed to be done," in the words of one mob member. The citizens of Atchison believed that they sent a loud and clear message to anyone attempting similar actions. This gang of thieves was summarily executed one by one with no due process or evidence, save for witness testimonials. We will never know how many were actually guilty nor how many actually died. This practice mostly petered out in Kansas by 1900, but six lynchings still took place between then and 1932.

5
THE PASSIONS OF WAR

Bullet Hole Ellis

It's unfortunate when history bestows a nickname on you due to an injury or birth defect. In literature, we might think of Captain Hook, so named because of the notorious replacement for his missing hand. In Russian history, there is Vasily the Cross-Eyed, grand prince of Moscow (1434–35). In the thirteenth century, Eric XI of Sweden earned the unfortunate nickname of Eric the Lisp and Lame, due to his talk and walk. My favorite is Justinian II, the seventh- and eighth-century Byzantine emperor dubbed the "Split-Nose" due to his nose being cut off the first time his enemies deposed him. It was replaced by a golden nose that he wore to conceal the damage. In Kansas, we have one character with a name to rival all of those: Abraham "Bullet Hole" Ellis.

Born in Green County, Ohio, in 1815, Ellis spent his early years as a successful teacher and farmer. He moved with his family to Miami County, Kansas, in September 1857, at the height of the Bleeding Kansas era. No fence-sitter, he presented himself as a firm and proud abolitionist and even befriended firebrand John Brown. Working with Brown as a trusted lieutenant and friend during these Border War years, Ellis and his younger brother, John, often spent the night away from home to keep the rest of the family safe in case they were targeted by proslavery men. Living just six miles from the Missouri border and having a strong stance on the slavery issue

Abraham "Bullet Hole" Ellis, who was shot by Quantrill. *Courtesy of Kansas Historical Society.*

took a lot of guts at this time. Staying at home might mean someone had to guard the house all night in case of attack.

In October 1858, Ellis was elected to the Kansas territorial legislature and later served as superintendent of public instruction and as a Miami County commissioner. The following December, he won another election to be a representative in the first state legislature. While working as superintendent, Ellis had authorization to grant teaching certificates. In 1860, one specific man, William C. Quantrill, earned one of these certificates to teach school in Stanton.

When the Civil War broke out, Ellis served as quartermaster for Lane's Brigade and busily brought aid to Kansas for the war effort. On March 7, 1862, while en route to Fort Leavenworth from Fort Scott, he stayed the night near the Johnson-Miami County lines at a rooming house owned by a man named Treacle. At sunrise, the homeowner woke everyone with a shrill cry of, "The bushwhackers are coming!" Shots rang out around the property, and Treacle and a man named Whitaker were shot dead. Another man, Tuttle, fell as Ellis jumped from his bed. Ellis had just put on a fur cap, and he peered out of the window just as William Quantrill aimed his pistol at it. The bullet passed through his cap and directly into his skull.

When he went into the house after it was pacified, Quantrill recognized Ellis from their interactions with the teaching certificate and expressed regret for hitting him. "You're not the kind of man I was looking for, I'm damned sorry," said Quantrill. He prevented any more harm to come to him from the other bushwhackers. Ellis was allowed to keep his horses and some groceries, though the men took some of his money. When the group left, Ellis was still alive, though he had a bullet lodged in his forehead.

Daguerreotype of antislavery crusader John Brown, 1850. *Courtesy of Library of Congress.*

Quantrill's bullet sat against the lining of Ellis's brain for three days, until it could be surgically removed, along with pieces of the shattered skull. The bullet and twenty-seven bone pieces were extracted with little difficulty, and the surgeon could even see Ellis's brain through the hole. After just five months, Ellis was completely healed, but that hole in his head would last the rest of his life. In September 1863, he was commissioned as a first lieutenant in the Fifteenth Kansas Company and served in this capacity to the end of the war.

As for Quantrill, his bloodiest attack on Kansas was yet to come. On August 21, 1863, he and three hundred to four hundred pro-Confederate raiders attacked a defenseless Lawrence, Kansas, and executed 164 men and boys. Lawrence had been a leading town in the fight against slavery since the Bleeding Kansas days and was in utter ruins after the attack. Quantrill was ambushed by Union soldiers in Kentucky and killed in June 1865.

As for Abraham, "Bullet Hole" Ellis became his nickname for the last twenty-three years of his life, and he died in Elk Falls, Kansas, on March

Left: James W. Perrine, one of the 164 Lawrencians killed in the Quantrill Raid. *Courtesy of Library of Congress*.

Below: Ruins of Lawrence, Kansas, from *Harper's Weekly* on August 21, 1863, after Quantrill's Raid. *Courtesy of Library of Congress*.

The Reign of Terror in Kanzas by Charles W. Briggs, 1856. Quantrill was the bloodiest final act of border warfare and terror dating back to the mid-1850s. *Courtesy of Kansas Historical Society.*

14, 1885. What happened to the ball and skull bits is a mystery to this day. Records at the Kansas Historical Society indicate that he sent them to the Army and Navy Medical Museum in Washington, D.C. This museum, however, never existed. It's likely that he meant the Army Medical Museum, which is now the National Museum of Health and Medicine of the Armed Forces Institute of Pathology. That museum says it does not have the items, though. Perhaps they reside on a forgotten shelf or in a drawer somewhere waiting to be rediscovered. The National Museum of Health and Medicine famously has Civil War general Daniel E. Sickles's amputated leg from Gettysburg. Maybe someday Ellis can get an exhibit next to his if those parts of his skull are ever found. It would be a fitting conclusion to a great story about a great nickname.

6
THIEVES

Dr. George Eaton:
The Dentist with an Exciting Hobby

The town of Columbus sits in the far southeast corner of the state and the locals enjoyed their relatively peaceful community of 2,300 people in 1899. The region grew various agricultural products and had a burgeoning mining industry of coal, zinc, oil, lead and salt. Crime was low, and the state's Bleeding Kansas and frontier cowboy days had run their course long ago. There was one small problem plaguing the town, though: a string of petty robberies and thefts.

Oftentimes in this era, the robbery of a home or business would be committed by a person traveling through town, so they could get away one step ahead of the law. Law enforcement would often head straight to nearby train stations to question suspicious-looking people boarding trains. But when reports came in of a few home burglaries in Columbus, the local sheriff came up empty-handed each time. The authorities realized that they were likely dealing with a local, as this problem kept happening. The town sat on edge as the random thefts and stickups happened out of the blue for years. Even local merchants could not avoid the crime spree—in March 1899, a thief relieved a local jewelry store of a significant number of its best pieces.

Local dentist Dr. George Eaton was a pillar of the community. He was respected by all and had attended to the dental needs of nearly everyone in town. The fact that he had money to spend was not a huge surprise, as he had a very industrious nature and worked long hours. His wife had recently been delighted by some jewelry that he had given her, and she proudly wore it out on the town. Embarrassingly enough for her, the police apprehended and questioned her, bringing in the jewelry merchant to identify the pieces she was wearing. Knowing nothing of the robbery, she said that they were gifts from her husband. It turned out that those were the recently stolen items, and the authorities headed to the Eaton home to question the doctor.

When they arrived at the home, the police arrested Dr. Eaton and were preparing to take him to the city jail as he gathered a few things to take with him. He seemed to acquiesce and was holding his child and speaking with the sheriff when, according to the *Abilene Weekly Reflector*, he "managed to escape by running past the guards with his baby in his arms, the guards not shooting for fear of killing the child." Eaton bolted out the door and managed to evade the authorities with the baby in tow. It's not clear exactly how he skipped town, but he managed to evade the authorities for days.

Like any good lawmen, the police questioned the railroad workers of every train coming and going from Columbus over the next few days. Witnesses and train employees described Dr. Eaton, and he was tracked down to Newton, Kansas, which was more than 180 miles away. When he was caught for the second time, he gave a full confession, admitting that he had committed all the mysterious robberies in Columbus. He was apparently thrilled by the "rush" of each crime he committed. Like many cases of petty crime, the perpetrator was caught through plain sloppiness. Let's hope he was a more careful dentist at least.

A Clever Horse Thief

Many stories about horse thieves from the nineteenth century follow a familiar pattern—man slips onto property at night, steals horse and rides off quietly without anyone noticing. It is the least risky method, and one usually took great care when stealing a horse. People often hanged for stealing horses, which were major investments for people back then. A poor farmer could be ruined by losing a horse in such a way. Occasionally, though, you hear of a brazen and hilarious ruse being perpetrated on an unwilling accomplice. One such incident happened in Fort Scott in August 1874.

Anti-Horse Thief Association's thirty-third annual meeting in Chanute, Kansas, in October 1914. Such gatherings were large affairs and showed the extensiveness of this organization. *Courtesy of Kansas Historical Society.*

A Sumner County man named James Long rode into Fort Scott on a warm August day. He made easy conversation around town and convinced a local citizen named Tannehill to lend him some money to help him pursue a horse thief. Having heard of some recent horse thefts, Mr. Tannehill "took it for granted that it was all right and advanced the amount desired," according to the *Fort Scott Daily Monitor*. As it turns out, Mr. Long was the horse thief himself and took on this persona to avoid suspicion. Not only did this throw people off his trail, but he amazingly got someone to give him money.

Long had borrowed a horse at a stable in Wichita and apparently "forgot to return it," according to the *Wichita Eagle*. Sedgwick County sheriff Pleasant H. Massy, hearing Long intended to reach Fort Scott, left town in pursuit. After making inquiries around town, he heard Tannehill's story. Feeling a fool, Tannehill and the local constable, Avery, pursued Long and caught up with him in Springfield, Missouri. By this time, he had somehow acquired three horses. All the group needed was the Kansas governor's permission to bring him back to the state.

Long was not only guilty of horse stealing but also of monetary theft. Massey brought him back to Wichita on September 1, 1874, after three weeks on the chase. He returned to accolades, and the *Wichita Eagle* praised him, saying, "Sheriff Massey seldom if ever fails to get his man when he goes for him. He returned a few days since with Long, who will have justice meted

out to him we trust." Horse theft meant such serious business that the sheriff even deputized his son to take over while he was gone. This goes to show that the crime constituted more than simple monetary theft; otherwise, he would have been tried in Fort Scott. Long got three years for his crime, and Massey delivered Long to the state penitentiary in late September.

On an ironic note, Long pulled his great stunt in Fort Scott, the place where the highly influential Anti-Horse Thief Association was founded in 1859. This vigilance society eventually spread over many states and helped farmers and horse owners share information on such thefts and apprehend suspects. Then again, Long wasn't going to let anything like that slow him down.

A Member of the James-Younger Gang Laid Low by a Farmer on Break

One of the most notorious outlaws in American history was Jesse James, the infamous Missourian who led the James-Younger Gang in numerous train, stagecoach and bank robberies across several states. Though he grew up near Kansas, in far-western Missouri, his gang rarely operated there since Kansas was full of former Jayhawkers and Union veterans. If they did enter Kansas, they would perform quick holdups right over the border, then head back to the safety of Missouri. There were few safe places to lay low and an unfriendly populace to deal with in Kansas. The

Right: Jesse James, 1882. *Courtesy of Library of Congress.*

Below: Jesse James's 1873 model .44 Hopkins and Allen Pistol. This was used in many train robberies. *Courtesy of Library of Congress.*

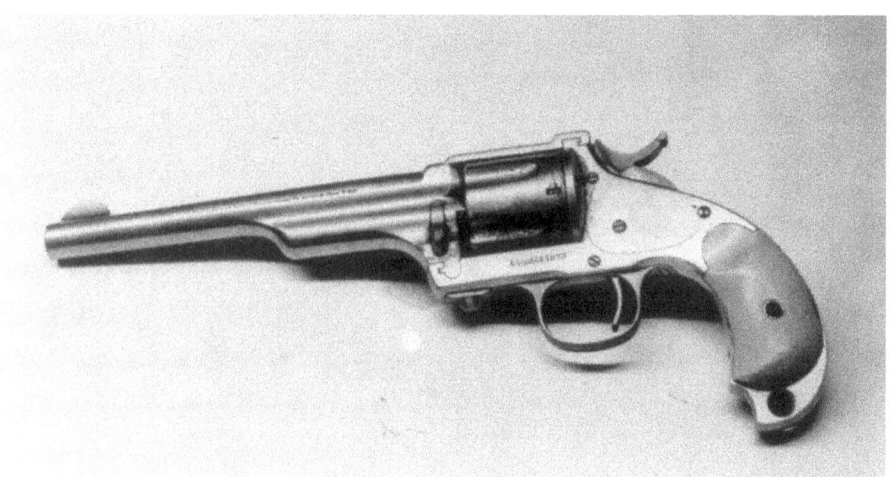

gang did jump the state line for a major train robbery, and when it was all said and done, a member of the gang was taken out by a crack shot farmer harvesting his crop.

In December 1874, after nearly eight years of increasingly successful robberies and holdups, the notorious Jesse James gang had set their sights on a Kansas Pacific train that was heading west from Kansas City. They knew that the train held a Wells Fargo safe that was likely full of money and valuables and decided to intercept it in the small town of Muncie, which was twelve miles west of the border. Arriving in Muncie before the train was scheduled to pass, the gang seized local railroad workers at gunpoint and forced them to pile wooden ties across the tracks. They also ordered a local general store owner to flag down the approaching train.

The train stopped as expected, and the masked gang immediately boarded the baggage car. The company messenger knew the safe's code and was ordered to open it for them. Inside was a bonanza of a haul, with $18,000 in cash and $5,000 in gold, as well as random personal jewelry and other goods stored for safekeeping. Having a certain code of honor, the messenger was given a gold watch that belonged to him. They preferred to rob from the faceless rich than the everyday citizen. When they rode away, they saluted the train workers and said, "Goodbye, boys. No hard feelings! We have taken nothing from you."

This train heist was a major coup for the gang, as $23,000 in 1874 is equivalent to more than $500,000 in modern currency. Wells Fargo, the Kansas Pacific Railroad and the State of Kansas all joined forces to offer a monetary reward for any information on the thieves and their whereabouts. By pure luck, one member of the gang brought himself down through his own stupidity. William "Bud" McDaniel, a brother of another James Gang member, ran afoul of the Kansas City Police a few days after the robbery for "rowdy behavior and public drunkenness." He was in high spirits and was spending wildly. Police found more than $1,000 on him, as well as jewelry from the safe, four revolvers and more than seventy cartridges.

Since Kansas City was friendlier to the James Gang—McDaniel was drinking with the chief of police earlier that day—it was decided to send McDaniel to Lawrence to wait for trial. Many officials and policemen in Kansas City feared the James Gang and dreaded sending their prisoner across state lines and into the hands of the Kansans. McDaniel escaped from the Douglas County jail on June 27, 1875, and he and three other escapees took off with horses, weapons and ammunition. The jail could not have botched this any worse.

Organizing a posse, the Douglas County deputy sheriff quickly tracked the escapees to a Kansas River oxbow lake called Lakeview, a few miles northwest of Lawrence. A local farmer named Louis Beurman had been harvesting all day that Monday and heard from a local constable that the men were nearby. Heading to his house, he grabbed his old squirrel rifle and set off to look for the fugitives. Seeing the men in an open space near some woods about a quarter of a mile from his house, he told the *Lawrence Republican-Journal*,

> *I saw the two men....They saw me at the same time, and McDaniels slipped from his horse and brought his gun to his shoulder. I took quick aim and fired. He felt the shot and almost fell forward on his face, but recovered himself immediately, pulling the trigger at me, the ball whistling over my head. Then he mounted, and together the two men dashed into the woods.*

Hit in the lower bowels, McDaniel stumbled to a local farmhouse as the other escapees fled. The residents informed the sheriff, and he was returned to the jail. A doctor inspected him and concluded that he wouldn't recover. McDaniel kept his lips sealed and refused to give up the other members of the gang before he died a few hours later.

The James Gang continued for nearly another decade before Jesse was shot and killed by a new gang recruit, Robert Ford, on April 3, 1882. Some

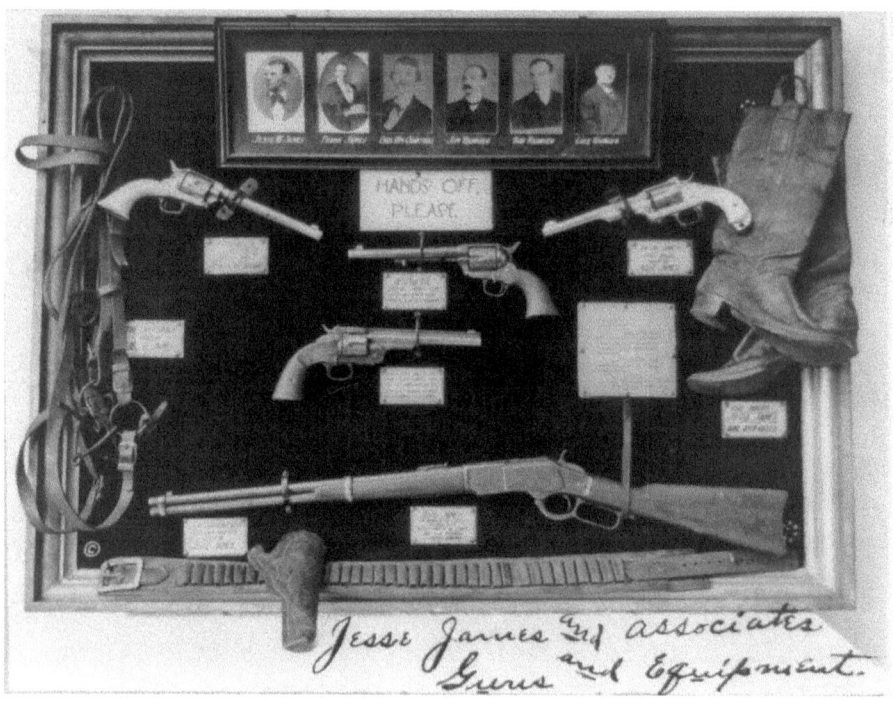

Collection of Jesse James and his associates' guns and equipment. *Courtesy of Library of Congress.*

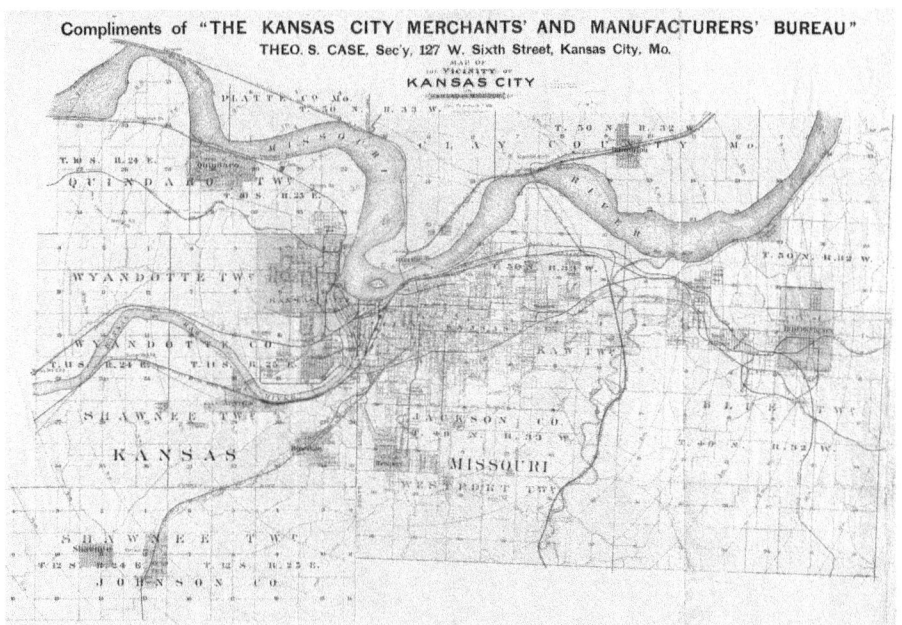

Map of Kansas City, Kansas, and Kansas City, Missouri, in 1880. It was in this landscape that the James Gang could raid into Kansas and slip back to relative safety in Missouri. *Courtesy of New York Public Library.*

think of Jesse as a Robin Hood figure, but there's no evidence that he did anything with the money he stole other than keep it for himself and his gang. He remains a legendary figure, and the old squirrel gun that felled McDaniel was donated to the Kansas Historical Society in 1958 by a nephew of Louis Beurman. It's an interesting artifact of a time when a member of a notorious gang was laid low by a farmer on break from his day's work.

7
CON ARTISTS

Lucien Ayer and Wildcat Banks

In the fall of 1854, an enterprising New Englander named Lucien Ayer boarded a train in his home state of New Hampshire and headed west to the newly opened Kansas Territory. Many people from Massachusetts, Vermont and New Hampshire headed there at this time to help settle it as a free state. With the question up in the air as to whether Kansas would be a slave or free state, many northern abolitionists and southern slaveholders and their supporters began flocking to the new territory in droves. Ayer had a different reason for coming, and it involved a very peculiar nineteenth-century scam.

When Kansas Territory opened for settlement, new residents faced many unique and unpredictable challenges. Not only were there food, water and weather conditions to grapple with, but politically explosive differences over slavery also drove wedges between many neighbors. In this chaotic era, getting goods and services for one's business, farm or family was tricky because there was very little actual money out there to use to buy goods. With anti- and proslavery forces at such bitter, and often violent, odds, the territory could not pass a constitution and regulate itself. Whichever side began organizing faced immediate branding as illegitimate by the other side; thus, commercial anarchy reigned.

Today, we have a common U.S. currency that the Treasury Department regulates. You can take your dollar from New York and spend it in Los

Angeles or anywhere. Back then, though, no national currency existed that could be regulated by the federal government. Poorer and more rural people often didn't even use money at all. They would barter goods and services with each other to get by, sometimes trading goods like chickens for clothing, with the value of each item haggled and negotiated. If money was used, it was often presented in a variety of ways, such as coins from other states or nations, personally crafted silver coins, property deeds and even small bits of gold or gold dust. Using paper money was almost unheard of because it didn't have intrinsic value to most people. They greatly mistrusted these paper notes because they basically meant nothing if there wasn't a guarantee of value behind it.

Paper currency could be printed and issued by any group, bank or organization and could be used as far as people trusted it. Between the 1830s and 1860s, known as the Free Banking Era, banks were regulated by the states only, and the regulation, if it happened at all, was largely infrequent and ineffective. In Kansas's case, it wasn't happening at all. But people needed money in this new land, and they bartered just about anything to get their hands on paper money if it meant they could use it to purchase goods. Desperate people would often trade goods and services to get their hands on some of this money.

This is the situation our plucky New Englander Lucien Ayer waltzed into in Leavenworth that fall of 1854. He announced that he was opening a bank with several partners and printed a number of wildcat notes that weren't guaranteed. His notes looked very official. They said "Kansas Ft. Leavenworth Merchants Bank" on the front and were decorated with designs of George Washington, an eagle and other elaborate images. The local press was skeptical of him, but that was not enough to stop him from slipping back east and distributing his notes as the bank president that he was. He conned several Kansas-bound people in Boston and New York out of their goods and services, and none of them ever got a dime for their worthless notes because his bank was never actually established. As they arrived in Kansas to use their new currency, they were shocked to learn from the locals that the bank never existed.

Plenty of wildcat banks popped up during this era in remote and rural areas, and it was very difficult, if not impossible, to have their notes redeemed anywhere else. The term "wildcat" hails from Michigan, where a bank once issued worthless notes with the image of a wildcat on them. The operators could run their cons without competition or interference from more reputable banks or authorities. There are even colorful stories of some of these wildcat banks leaving their safes partly open behind the counter to show some of the cash on hand, giving depositors a glimpse of their solvency and legitimacy as holders of wealth. In reality, they would often display a crate or barrel filled with grain or nails, with a thin layer of coins on top to create the illusion of deep reserves of currency.

A number of these banks went belly-up in this era, and people lost large amounts of money—sometimes everything they had—by putting their faith in unsecured notes. By 1858, the territorial legislature finally required banks to have $2,500 in coins on hand and to deposit at least $25,000 in U.S. or state bonds to demonstrate their solvency. Many banks had either no securities or inadequate amounts. With the creation of the U.S. Federal Reserve in 1913, the monetary system was finally under a centralized control.

The con artist is always drawn to places of disorder, hoping to cash in on the confusion and desperation of people. Lucien Ayer was just one of many who took advantage of the Wild West atmosphere of Kansas at the time. The locals were incensed when his "shin-plasters" (worthless notes similar to ones Revolutionary War troops put in their boots for comfort) still floated around town after he left. What happened to him and his con anyway, you might wonder. The *Boston Chronicle* reported on January 1855,

> *A New Hampshire man by the name of Lucien Ayer, of Plaistow, in that State, and more recently President of a "wild-cat" bank in Kansas, whose bills he had been getting rid of at a rapid rate in New York and Boston... was recently arrested at Plaistow, to which place he had lately returned with his wife, on an old charge of arson, for which he had been tried three years ago.*

It looks like his criminal actions were diverse, and one of them caught up with him. The citizens of Leavenworth laughed it up...all the way to the bank.

BEN HODGES:
A CON MAN EVEN A MOTHER COULD LOVE

Many liars, thieves, cattle rustlers and con artists have passed through the Sunflower State over the years. Some were hanged or ended up in prison, while others got away scot-free. It takes a special kind of person to inhabit all the qualities generally despised by Kansans—dishonesty, lawlessness and thievery—and still become a beloved character. There is no greater example in this state's history than cowboy Ben Hodges.

Born in 1856 in Texas of mixed Mexican/Castilian and African American ancestry, a young Ben was rejected by his mother after years of disdain from her family for his racial heritage. Not only was he a mixed-race child of divorce in nineteenth-century Texas, but he also had a peculiar slow shuffle to his walk, which could have been caused by rheumatism or an unexplained injury. To put it simply, Ben had some major challenges working against him. Since a good 25 percent of cowboys from the 1860s to 1880s were black, Hodges wasn't too much of an anomaly when he left Texas for Dodge City at sixteen years old in 1872. Working as a drover for famed Kansas cattleman W.D. "Doc" Barton, he came to the town on his way to Great Bend and decided to stay.

Rumors circulated that he refused to head back to Texas because he had killed a man down there. He stuck around Kansas and soon fell in with some horse and cattle thieves. One of his favorite cons was to steal cattle, then "find" them and collect the reward money offered by the owners. This line of work was preferable to him because the work of a drover was too dirty, lonely and difficult for his tastes.

Always willing to look for a new angle, he learned of a supposed Spanish land grant for a property outside of Dodge City. He was a master forger, and he created a series of documents to support his claim that he was the beneficiary of said land. Playing fast and loose with his Mexican ancestry and Spanish genealogy, he even conned a new bank president in town to believe his story and extend him not only a large line of credit but also, amazingly, a letter of recommendation. With the large loans that followed, he was able to rub elbows with Dodge City's wealthier citizens. Ultimately, this con faltered, and he couldn't reasonably prove his claim when there was a large fire at the Wright, Beverly and Company Store, and the rightful documents to the land claim were discovered in a vault.

As with any good con man, Hodges was great at charming people and talking his way out of trouble. When he was caught stealing a herd of dairy cows, he was arrested and put on trial for cattle theft. As he was destitute, Hodges had no other choice but to represent himself. Having intimately known this notoriously dishonest local character, the people of Dodge City thought for sure this was going to be the case that sent him to prison.

The old charmer went to court and gave a two-hour speech to the jury. Not only did he endear them with his humor, but he also entertained them with his ridiculous posturing. "What me," he said. "The descendant of old grandees of Spain, the owner of a land grant embracing millions of acres, the owner of gold mines and villages and towns situated on that grant of which I am sole owner, to steal a miserable, miserly lot of old cows? Why, the idea is absurd. No, gentlemen. I think too much of the race of men from which I sprang, to disgrace their memory." The jury was so entertained and laughed so much that they acquitted him. Conveniently, some days after the end of the trial, the "missing" cows somehow returned home on their own.

Ben went on and continued to be a local card shark, schemer and attempted swindler of pretty much any and every citizen of Dodge City. As time went on, he was seen less as a bad man and more as a harmless, but still untrustworthy, character. As his situation was always quite modest—he lived in a hut that he built himself—many shopkeepers would look the other way when he shoplifted from their stores. Some stores even let him fill his basket with what he needed. The police even warmed to him, giving him a nonworking pistol and making him an honorary assistant deputy. As he got older, he received gifts on holidays, including a flock of ducks from well-wishing townsfolk one Thanksgiving.

In 1929, Ben died after a long illness at the age of seventy-three. His hut burned to the ground shortly before this, but a friend of his took care of him until the end. His funeral was well attended, with more than two hundred people filling Sacred Heart Catholic Church in Dodge City. Most poor citizens and county dependents were given pine coffins for burial, but town residents pitched in to get him a nice casket. His friends buried him in Maple Grove Cemetery, along with many other cowboys from the era who he had likely successfully conned during his many years. One friend was quoted as saying, "We buried him there for a good reason—we wanted him where we could keep a good eye on him."

His tombstone, paid for by the Ford County Historical Society and private donors in 1965, reads, "Ben Hodges, Self-styled Desperado, a Colorful Pioneer." Hodges is remembered today as one of the most famous black cowboys—up there with Nat "Deadwood Dick" Love and rodeo celebrity Bill Pickett. It's quite a feat that a man who had so many financial and racial challenges could become a notorious thief and swindler and somehow not only survive in a place like Dodge City but also become beloved by the very people he always tried to con.

BIBLIOGRAPHY

Albert, D. Kendall. "North from Texas: The Long Cattle Drives, as Told by the Trail Drivers." *Western Brand Book* 43, no. 1 (1899): 3–6, 17–20.
Allen, Judy. "Children on the Overland Trails." *Overland Journal* 12 (Spring 1994): 2–11.
Alley, J. Mark. *The Violent Years: The Founding of a Kansas Town*. Hillsboro, KS: Prairie Books, 1993.
Ambler, Cathy. "A Place Not Entirely of Sadness and Gloom: Oak Hill Cemetery and the Rural Cemetery Movement." *Kansas History* 15 (Winter 1992–93): 240–53.
———. "Small Historic Sites in Kansas: Merging Artifactual Landscapes and Community Values." *Great Plains Quarterly* 15 (Winter 1995): 33–48.
Anderson, George L., Terry H. Harmon and Virgil W. Dean. *History of Kansas*. Lawrence: Division of Continuing Education, University of Kansas, 1987.
———, eds. *History of Kansas: Selected Readings*. Lawrence: Division of Continuing Education, University of Kansas, 1987.
Andreas, Alfred Thayer. *The History of the State of Kansas*. With William G. Cutler. 2 vols. Chicago: A.T. Andreas, 1883.
Argersinger, Peter H. *The Limits of Agrarian Radicalism: Western Populism and American Politics*. Lawrence: University Press of Kansas, 1995.
———. "No Rights on this Floor: Third Parties and the Institutionalization of Congress [Populism]." *Journal of Interdisciplinary History* 22 (Spring 1992): 655–90.
Armitage, Merle. *Homage to the Santa Fe: The Many Facets of Big Time Railroading*. Hawthorne, CA: Omni Publications, 1973.

BIBLIOGRAPHY

Austin, John Sands. "Convergence in the Plains." PhD diss., University of Nebraska–Lincoln, 1996.

Averill, Thomas Fox, ed. *What Kansas Means to Me: Twentieth Century Writers on the Sunflower State.* Lawrence: University Press of Kansas, 1990.

Bader, Robert Smith. *Hayseeds, Moralizers, and Methodists: The Twentieth-Century Image of Kansas.* Lawrence: University Press of Kansas, 1988.

Bair, Bruce. *Good Land: My Life as a Farm Boy.* South Royalton, VA: Steerforth Press, 1997.

Ball, Larry D. "The United States Army and the Big Springs, Nebraska, Train Robbery of 1877." *Journal of the West* 34 (January 1995): 34–45.

Barton, O.S. *Three Years with Quantrill: A True Story Told by His Scout John McCorkle.* With notes by Albert Castel and commentary by Herman Hattaway. Norman: University of Oklahoma Press, 1992. First published in 1915.

Biggers, Don Hampton. *Buffalo Guns and Barbed Wire: Two Frontier Accounts.* Edited by Lawrence H. and Nancy Larsen. Lubbock: Texas Tech University Press, 1991.

Blackburn, Forrest R., et al. *Kansas and the West: Bicentennial Essays in Honor of Nyle H. Miller.* Topeka: Kansas State Historical Society, 1976.

Blackmar, Frank W. *Kansas: A Cyclopedia of State History.* Vol 1. Chicago. Standard Publishing Company, 1912.

Blair, William Alan, ed. *A Politician Goes to War: The Civil War Letters of John White Geary.* University Park: Pennsylvania State University Press, 1995.

Blevins, Winfred, ed. *Dictionary of the American West.* New York: Facts on File, 1993.

Bollig, M. Joseph. "Frank Motz and the First Eleven Years of the *Hays* (Kansas) *Daily News*—1929 to 1939." Master's thesis, University of Kansas, 1988.

Brackman, Barbara. "How Kansas Gave Texas the Boot." *Kansas Heritage* 2 (Autumn 1994): 34–38.

Bradley, Glenn D. *The Story of the Santa Fe.* 2nd ed. Palmdale, CA: Omni Publications, 1995.

Branyan, Helen B. "Medical Charlatanism: The Goat Gland Wizard of Milford, Kansas." *Journal of Popular Culture* 25 (Summer 1991): 31–37.

Bright, John D., ed. *Kansas: The First Century.* 4 vols. New York: Lewis Historical Publishing, 1956.

Brown, Dee. *Wondrous Times on the Frontier.* Little Rock, AR: August House Publishers, 1991.

Burke, W.S. *Official Military History of Kansas Regiments During the War for the Suppression of the Great Rebellion.* Ottawa: Kansas Heritage Press, 1995.

Burton, Bob. "The Early Days of the Southern Kansas Railway of Texas." *Panhandle-Plains Historical Review* 64 (1991): 86–98.

Call, Leland E. "Agricultural History of Kansas." Prepared for the Bellows-Reeves company [1921].

BIBLIOGRAPHY

Campney, Brent M.S. "Ever Since the Hanging of Oliphant: Lynching and the Suppression of Mob Violence in Topeka, Kansas." *Great Plains Quarterly* 33, no. 2 (Spring 2013).

Carney, James E. "The Freudians Come to Kansas: Menninger, Freud, and the Emigre Psychoanalysts." *Kansas History* 16 (Summer 1993): 78–93.

———. "Karl A. Menninger's Psychoanalytic Odyssey: Karl A. Menninger, Smith Ely Jelliffe, and the European Emigre Psychoanalysts." Master's thesis, Bowling Green State University, 1986.

Carson, Gerald. "The Great Plains Revisited." *Timeline* 8 (December 1991–January 1992): 46–51.

Carver, Frances Grace. "From Sanctuary to Saloon: Carry A. Nation and the Religious Ethos of the Midwestern United States, 1850-1900." PhD diss., Princeton Theological Seminary, 1997.

Castel, Albert. *Civil War Kansas: Reaping the Whirlwind, the Authorized Edition with a New Preface*. Lawrence: University Press of Kansas, 1997.

Cecil-Fronsman, Bill. "'Advocate the Freedom of White Men, As Well As That of the Negroes': The Kansas Free State and Antislavery Westerns in Territorial Kansas." *Kansas History* 20 (Summer 1997): 102–15.

———. "'Death to all Yankees and Traitors in Kansas': The Squatter Sovereign and the Defense of Slavery in Kansas." *Kansas History* 16 (Spring 1993): 22–33.

Chinn, Jennie A. *The Kansas Journey*. Salt Lake City, UT: Gibbs Smith, 2005.

Cigler, Allan, and Burdett Loomis. "Kansas: Two-Party Competition in a One-Party State." In *Party Realignment and State Politics*. Columbus: Ohio State University Press, 1992.

Clements, John. *Kansas Facts: A Comprehensive Look at Kansas Today, County by County, Flying the Colors*. Dallas, TX: Clements Research II, 1990.

Connelley, William E. *A Standard History of Kansas and Kansans*. 5 vols. Chicago: Lewis Publishing, 1918.

Crouch, Barry Alan. "In Search of Union: Amos A. Lawrence and the Coming of the Civil War." PhD diss., University of New Mexico, 1970.

Dastrup, Boyd L. *A Centennial History: The U.S. Army Command and General Staff College*. Manhattan KS: Sunflower University Press, 1982.

Davis, Kenneth S. *Kansas: A Bicentennial History*. New York: W.W. Norton, 1976.

Delano, Patti, and Cathy Johnson. *Kansas: Off the Beaten Path*. Chester, CT: Globe Pequot Press, 1991.

Dick, Everett. *The Sod-House Frontier, 1854–1890: A Social History of the Northern Plains from the Creation of Kansas & Nebraska to the Admission of the Dakotas*. New York: Appelton Century, 1937.

Dickenson, James R. *Home on the Range: A Century on the High Plains*. New York: Scribner, 1995.

Drees, James D. *Gunfighters of Ellis County*. Hays, KS: *Hays Daily News*, 1992.

Bibliography

Dykstra, Robert R. "Field Notes: Overdosing on Dodge City." *Western Historical Quarterly* 27 (Winter 1996): 505–14.

Egloff, Fred R. "Lawmen and Gunmen: A Contrasting View of the Old Peace Officers in Kansas and Texas." *Journal of the West* 34 (January 1995): 19–26.

Emmons, David M. "Constructed Province: History of the Making of the Last American West." *Western Historical Quarterly* 25 (Winter 1994): 437–59.

Etulain, Richard W., ed. *The American West in the Twentieth Century: A Bibliography.* Norman: University of Oklahoma Press, 1994.

Fellman, Michael. "Julia Louisa Lovejoy Goes West." *Western Humanities Review* 31 (Summer 1977): 227–42.

Fitzgerald, Dan. "Faded Dreams: Ghost Towns of Kansas." *Kansas Heritage* 1 (Summer 1993): 27–9.

———. *Faded Dreams: More Ghost Towns of Kansas.* Lawrence: University Press of Kansas, 1994.

Ford County Historical Society. *Dodge City and Ford County, Kansas (1870–1920)—Pioneer Histories and Stories.* Dodge City, KA: Society, 1996.

Frazier, Harriet C. *Lynchings in Kansas, 1850s–1932.* Jefferson, NC: McFarland, 2015.

Frehill-Rowe, Lisa M. "Postbellum Race Relations and Rural Land Tenure: Migration of Blacks and Whites to Kansas and Nebraska, 1870–1890." *Social Forces* 72 (September 1993): 77–92.

Gilmore, Donald L. "Total War on the Missouri Border." *Journal of the West* 35 (July 1996): 70–80.

Goodrich, Thomas. *Black Flag: Guerrilla Warfare on the Western Border, 1861–1865.* Bloomington: Indiana University Press, 1995.

Grafton, John. *The American West in the Nineteenth Century: 255 Illustrations from "Harper's Weekly" and Other Contemporary Sources.* New York: Dover Publications, 1992.

Grey, Alan H. "Roads, Railways, and Mountains: Getting Around in the West." *Journal of the West* 33 (July 1994): 35–44.

Griekspoor, Phyllis Jacobs, and Beccy Tanner. *Kansas: The Prairie Spirit—History People Stories.* Carson City, NV: Grace Dangberg Foundation, 2000.

Harris, Charles F. "Catalyst for Terror: The Collapse of the Women's Prison in Kansas City." *Missouri Historical Review* 89 (April 1995): 290–306.

Haywood, C. Robert. "Cowboy Nicknames in Nineteenth-Century Great Plains Cattle Country." *Heritage of the Great Plains* 29 (Spring/Summer 1996): 14–22.

———. "Personal Banking in Cattle Town Dodge City." In *Prairie Scout.* Vol 6. Manhattan: Kansas Corral of the Westerners, 1996, 13–22.

Heller, Francis H. *The Kansas State Constitution: A Reference Guide.* Westport, CT: Greenwood Publishing Group, 1992.

Herklotz, Hildegarde Rose. "Jayhawkers in Missouri, 1858–1863." *Missouri Historical Review* 17 (April 1923): 266–84.

Bibliography

History Book Committee. *At Home in Ellis County, Kansas, 1867–1992*. 2 vols. Hays, KS: Ellis County Historical Society, 1991.

Howes, Charles C. *This Place Called Kansas*. Norman: University of Oklahoma Press, 1952.

Hoy, Jim. *Cowboys and Kansas: Stories from the Tallgrass Prairie*. Norman: University of Oklahoma Press, 1994.

Hutson, Cecil Kirk. "Texas Fever in Kansas, 1866–1930." *Agricultural History* 68 (Winter 1994): 74–104.

Ise, John. *Sod and Stubble: The Unabridged and Annotated Edition*. With additional material by Von Rothenberger. Lawrence: University Press of Kansas, 1996.

James, John T. *The Benders in Kansas*. Pittsburg, KS: Mostly Books, 1913.

Kellow, Margaret M.R. "'For the Sake of Suffering Kansas': Lydia Maria Child, Gender, and the Politics of the 1850s." *Journal of Women's History* 5 (Fall 1993): 32–49.

King, Marsha K. "Guardians of the Plains: Military Forts in Kansas." *Kansas Heritage* 4 (Winter 1996): 4–8.

Knoblock, Frieda Elizabeth. "The Culture of Wilderness: Agriculture, Colonization, and the American West." Vol 1 and 2. PhD diss., University of Minnesota, 1994.

Lacalle, Jose Maria. "Wild Bill Hickok." *Historia* 16 (August 1996): 119–25.

Lambertson, John Mark. "Last Writes: History on Headstones." *Kansas Heritage* 2 (Spring 1994): 11–13.

Lee, Wayne C. *Deadly Days in Kansas*. Caldwell, ID: Caxton Printers, 1997.

Leslie, Edward E. *The Devil Knows How to Ride: The True Story of William Clarke Quantrill and His Confederate Raiders*. New York: Random House, 1996.

Maki, Thomas N. *Men of Franklin: Franklin Citizens in the Kansas Free-State Conflict: Their Lives and Times*. Hopedale, MA: Birch Hill Associates, 1996.

McChristian, Douglas. *The U.S. Army in the West, 1870–1880: Uniforms, Weapons, and Equipment*. Norman: University of Oklahoma Press, 1995.

Merrill, Irving. "The Civil War in the West: The 1864 Trail Season." *Overland Journal* 9 (Winter 1991): 15–27.

Miller, Nyle H., and Joseph W. Snell. *Great Gunfighters of the Kansas Cowtowns, 1867–1886*. Lincoln: University of Nebraska Press, 1967.

———. *Why the West Was Wild: A Contemporary Look at the Antics of Some Highly Publicized Kansas Cowtown Personalities*. Topeka: Kansas State Historical Society, 1963.

Miner, H. Craig. *Kansas: The History of the Sunflower State, 1854–2000*. Lawrence: University Press of Kansas in association with Kansas State Historical Society, 2005.

Napier, Rita, ed. *A History of the Peoples of Kansas*. Lawrence: University of Kansas Division of Continuing Education, 1985.

Otero, Miguel Antonio. *My Life on the Frontier, 1864–1882: Incidents and Characters of the Period When Kansas, Colorado, and New Mexico Were Passing Through the Last of Their Wild and Romantic Years*. New York: Press of Pioneers, 1935.

BIBLIOGRAPHY

Patterson, Richard M. *Historical Atlas of the Outlaw West*. New York: Johnson Books, 1984.

Peters, Robert M. *Our Kansas Heritage: A Memoir of the 1920s and 1930s*. Arkansas City, KS: Gilliland Printing, 1993.

Peterson, John M., ed. "From Border War to Civil War: More Letters of Edward and Sarah Fitch, 1855–1863, Part I." *Kansas History* 20 (Spring 1997): 2–21.

———. "From Border War to Civil War: More Letters of Edward and Sarah Fitch, 1855–1863, Part II." *Kansas History* 20 (Summer 1997): 68–85.

Peterson, Roger S. "Wyatt Earp: Man Versus Myth." *American History Illustrated* 29 (August 1994): 54–61, 68–70.

Phillips, Charles, and Alan Axelrod, eds. *Encyclopedia of the American West*. New York: Macmillan, 1996.

Pierson, Michael D., ed. "'A War of Extermination:' A Newly Uncovered Letter by Julia Louisa Lovejoy, 1856." *Kansas History* 16 (Summer 1993): 120–23.

Richmond, Robert W. *Kansas: Land of Contrast*. 4th ed. Wheeling, IL: Harlan Davidson, 1999.

Rogers, Richard D. "The Story of Brave Kansans." *Kansas History* 18 (Winter 1995/1996): 258–69.

Rosa, Joseph G. *Wild Bill Hickok: The Man and His Myth*. Lawrence: University Press of Kansas, 1996.

Savage, William W., Jr., ed. *Cowboy Life: Reconstructing an American Myth*. Niwot: University Press of Colorado, 1993.

Schruben, Francis W. "The Wizard of Milford: Dr. J.R. Brinkley and Brinkleyism." *Kansas History* 14 (Winter 1991–92): 226–45.

Schultz, Duane. *Quantrill's War: The Life and Times of William Clarke Quantrill*. New York: St. Martin's Press, 1996.

Self, Huber, and Stephen E. White. "One Hundred and Twenty Years of Population Change in Kansas." *Transactions of the Kansas Academy of Science* 89, no. 1–2 (1986): 10–22.

SenGupta, Gunja. "'A Model New England State:' Northeastern Antislavery in Territorial Kansas, 1854–1860." *Civil War History* 39 (March 1993): 31–46.

Sheets, Jeff. "Head 'Em Up, Move 'Em Out: The Legacy of the Chisholm Trail." *Kansas Heritage* 5 (Summer 1997): 4–8.

Shortridge, James R. *Peopling the Plains: Who Settled Where in Frontier Kansas*. Lawrence: University Press of Kansas, 1995.

Socolofsky, Homer E. *Kansas Governors*. Lawrence: University Press of Kansas, 1990.

Socolofsky, Homer E., and Huber Self. *Historical Atlas of Kansas*. 2nd ed. Norman: University of Oklahoma Press, 1989.

Socolofsky, Homer E., and Virgil W. Dean. *Kansas History: An Annotated Bibliography*. New York: Greenwood Press, 1992.

Stanley, Ellen May. *Cowboy Josh: Adventures of a Real Cowboy*. Newton, KS: Mennonite Press, 1996.

Bibliography

Stuewe, Paul K., ed. *Kansas Revisited: Historical Images and Perspectives.* Lawrence: University of Kansas Division of Continuing Education, 1990.

Takahashi, Yuko. "Frontier Children: Childhood Experiences in Kansas, 1860–1900." *American Review* 22 (March 1988): 170–91.

Tanner, Beccy. *Bear Grease, Builders and Bandits: The Men and Women of Wichita's Past.* Wichita, KS: Wichita Eagle and Beacon Publishing, 1991.

Thrapp, Dan L. *Encyclopedia of Frontier Biography.* Vol 4: Supplemental Volume. Spokane, WA: Arthur H. Clark Company, 1994.

Underwood, Larry D. *Abilene Lawmen: The Smith-Hickok Years, 1870–71.* Crete, NE. Dageforde Publishing, 1999.

Watts, Dale. "How Bloody Was Bleeding Kansas? Political Killings in Kansas Territory, 1854–1861." *Kansas History* 18 (Summer 1995): 116–29.

Webb, Dave. *399 Kansas Characters.* With illustrations by Phillip R. Buntin. Dodge City: Kansas Heritage Center, 1992.

Weir, William. *Written with Lead: Legendary American Gunfights and Gunfighters.* Hamden, CT: Archon, 1992.

Wheeler, David L. "Winter on the Cattle Range in Western Kansas, 1884–1886." *Kansas History* 15 (Spring 1992): 2–17.

Wilson, Paul E. "How the Law Came to Kansas." *Kansas History* 15 (Spring 1992): 18–35.

———. "Law on the Frontier." *Trail Guide* 5 (September 1960): 1–16.

Wilson, R.L. *The Peacemakers: Arms and Adventure in the American West.* New York: Random House, 1992.

Wilson, Sandy. "Able Marshal of Abilene." *Wild West Magazine.* February 1995.

Worster, Donald. *Under Western Skies.* New York: Oxford University Press, 1992.

Zornow, William Frank. *Kansas: A History of the Jayhawk State.* Norman: University of Oklahoma Press, 1957.

ABOUT THE AUTHOR

Adrian Zink is a native Kansan who has worked at a variety of historical institutions, including the Kansas Historical Society, UW–Milwaukee Archives and the National Press Club Library and Archives. He has a Bachelor of Arts in history and political science, a Master of Library Science and a Master of Arts in history. He currently works at the National Archives–Kansas City and teaches a class on Kansas history for the University of Kansas Osher Institute. Adrian lives in Overland Park, Kansas. His first book, *Hidden History of Kansas*, was published in 2017.

www.ingramcontent.com/pod-product-compliance
Lightning Source LLC
Chambersburg PA
CBHW040251170426
43191CB00018B/2378